The Constitution of
The State of New Mexico:
A Quick Reference Guide

Bootblack Budget Books
Copyright 2018 ©
ISBN-13: 978-1719410922
ISBN-10: 1719410925

Contents:

Preamble – Page 33

> **Article I: Name and Boundaries** – Page 34

Section 1. Name and Boundaries

Article II: Bill of Rights – Page 35

Section 1. Supreme Law of the Land

Section 2. Government By the People

Section 3. Sovereign and Independent State

Section 4. Inalienable Rights

Section 5. Treaty of Guadalupe Hidalgo Rights

Section 6. Right To Keep and Bear Arms

Section 7. Writ of Habeas Corpus

Section 8. Elections

Section 9. Military Subordination

Section 10. Searches and Seizures

Section 11. Religious Freedom

Section 12. Trial by Jury

Section 13. Bail; Excessive Fines; Cruel and Unusual Punishment

Section 14. Grand Jury; Information and Indictment; Rights of Accused

Section 15. Self-Incrimination; Double Jeopardy

Section 16. Treason

Section 17. Freedom of Speech and of the Press; Libel

Section 18. Due Process; Equal Protection; Sex Discrimination

Section 19. Ex Post Facto Law; Bill of Attainder; Obligation of Contract

Section 20. Eminent Domain

Section 21. Imprisonment For Debt Prohibited

Section 23. Construction of Constitutional Rights

Section 24. Rights of Crime Victims

Article III: Distribution of Powers – Page 43

Section 1. Separation of Departments; Establishment of Workers Compensation Body

Article IV: Legislative Department – Page 44

Section 1. Legislative Power; Referenda on Legislation

Section 2. Emergency Powers

Section 3. Composition of Legislature; Qualifications of Members

Section 4. Legislative Terms and Elections; Vacancies

Section 5. Regular Sessions

Section 6. Special Sessions; Extraordinary Sessions

Section 7. Quorum; Judge of Election and Qualifications of Members

Section 8. Call To Order; Presiding Officers

Section 9. Officers and Employees; Compensation

Section 10. Compensation of Members

Section 11. Rules of Procedure; Contempt, Disorderly Behavior; Expulsion of A Member

Section 12. Public Session; Journal of Proceedings

Section 13. Arrest Or Questioning of Members

Section 14. Adjournment

Section 15. Passage of Law By Bill; Enacting Clause; Readings

Section 16. Content and Form of Bills; Appropriations

Section 17. Passage of Bill

Section 18. Amendment and Revision of Law; Tax Laws

Section 19. Time Limitations On Introduction of Bills

Section 20. Enrollment and Signing of Bills; Interlineations

Section 21. Alteration or Theft of Bills

Section 22. Presentment to Governor; Approvals and Vetoes

Section 23. Effective Date of Laws

Section 24. Local and Special Laws

Section 25. Unauthorized or Invalid Acts of Officers

Section 26. Privileges, Immunities, and Franchises

Section 27. Compensation of Public Officers, Agents, or Contractors

Section 28. Members Involvement in Civil Offices and Contracts

Section 29. Laws Authorizing Indebtedness

Section 30. Public Monies and Appropriations

Section 31. Appropriations To Bodies Not Under the Control of the State

Section 32. Obligations and Liabilities

Section 33. Prosecution and Punishment Under Repealed Law

Section 34. Pending Cases

Section 35. Impeachment Power and Procedure

Section 36. Impeachment of Officers and Judges

Section 37. Railroad Transportation of Members

Section 38. Restraint of Trade

Section 39. Bribery and Solicitation

Section 40. Penalty for Bribery and Solicitation

Section 41. Compelling Testimony in Bribery and Solicitation Proceedings

Section 42. Interim Committees on Gubernatorial Appointments

Article V: Executive Department – Page 60

Section 1. Executive Department Composition

Section 2. Canvassing of Elections; Tie Votes

Section 3. Eligibility for Office

Section 4. Powers of the Governor

Section 5. Appointments; Vacancies in State Offices

Section 6. Reprieves and Pardons

Section 7. Succession To Office of Governor

Section 8. Lieutenant Governor; Senate Voting

Section 9. Accounts of and Reports By Executive Department and Public Institutions

Section 10. State Seal

Section 11. Commissions

Section 12. Compensation of Executive Officers

Section 13. Local Government Officers; Districting

Section 14. State Transportation Commission

Section 15. Heads of Cabinet-Level Departments Or Agencies; Appointment; Confirmation Or Reconfirmation

Section 16. Vacancy; Lieutenant Governor; Nomination

Section 17. State Ethics Commission Unofficial Classification Editorially Supplied by Thomson Reuters

Article VI: Judicial Department – Page 66

Section 1. Judicial Powers

Section 2. Supreme Court; Appellate Jurisdiction

Section 3. Supreme Court; Original Jurisdiction; Superintending Control Over Inferior Courts

Section 4. Supreme Court; Composition

Section 5. Supreme Court; Quorum and Judgment

Section 6. Supreme Court; Interested, Absent, Or Incapacitated Justice

Section 7. Supreme Court; Annual Term

Section 8. Supreme Court Justices; Qualifications

Section 9. Supreme Court; Employees

Section 10. Supreme Court; Number of Justices

Section 11. Supreme Court Justices; Compensation

Section 12. Judicial Districts; Judges

Section 13. District Courts; Jurisdiction

Section 13. District Courts; Jurisdiction

Section 14. District Judges; Qualifications

Section 15. District Judges; Designation; Disqualification

Section 16. District Courts; Number of Judges; Redistricting

Section 17. District Judges; Compensation

Section 18. Conflicts of Interest

Section 19. Nomination, Appointment, Or Election To Nonjudicial Office

Section 20. Writs and Processes

Section 21. Preliminary Examinations; Conservators of the Peace

Section 22. County Clerks

Section 23. Probate Court

Section 24. District Attorneys

Section 26. Magistrate Court

Section 27. Appeals

Section 27. Appeals

Section 28. Court of Appeals; Composition and Qualifications; Quorum

Section 29. Court of Appeals; Jurisdiction

Section 30. Fees Collected by Judicial Department

Section 31. Justices of the Peace

Section 32. Judicial Standards Commission

Section 33. Judicial Elections

Section 34. Vacancy of Judicial Office; Filing of Declaration of Candidacy

Section 35. Appellate Judges Nominating Commission

Section 36. District Court Judges Nominating Committee

Section 37. Metropolitan Court Judges Nominating Committee

Section 38. Chief Judges

Section 39. Creation of Public Defender Department and Public Defender Commission

Article VII: Elective Franchise – Page 81

Section 1. Voter Eligibility; Absentee Voting; School Elections; Registration

Section 2. Public Officer Qualifications; Discrimination

Section 3. Discrimination In Voting, Juror Selection, and Holding Office

Section 4. Residence

Section 5. Elections by Ballot; Runoff Elections; Number of Votes

Article VIII: Taxation and Revenue – Page 84

Section 1. Tangible Property; Valuation; Equal and Uniform Taxation

Section 2. Real or Personal Property Taxes

Section 3. Tax Exemptions

Section 4. Public Monies; Public Officer Profits; Investments

Section 5. Head of Family and Veteran Exemptions

Section 6. Real Property Assessments

Section 7. Judgments Against Local Governments or Officers

Section 8. Interstate Commerce, Exemption

Section 9. Tax Levies by Elected Governing Authority

Section 10. Severance Tax Permanent Fund

Section 15. Property Tax Exemption for Disabled Veteran

Section 16. Property Tax Exemption for Property of Veterans Organization Chartered by

Article IX: State, County and Municipal Indebtedness – Page 90

Section 1. Liabilities of Territory and Counties Assumed

Section 2. County Liability for Debt of Another County

Section 3. Bonds Issued to Pay Assumed Debts

Section 4. Bonds of Grant and Santa Fe Counties

Section 5. Laws Releasing County From Debt

Section 6. Militia Warrants

Section 7. State Indebtedness for Certain Purposes

Section 8. Restrictions on State Indebtedness

Section 9. Application of Borrowed Money

Section 10. County Indebtedness

Section 11. School District Indebtedness

Section 12. Local Government Indebtedness; Ordinances

Section 13. Local Government Debt Limitations

Section 14. Aid to Private Enterprise; Veterans Scholarship Program; Student Loans; Job Opportunities; Affordable Housing

Section 15. Refunding Bonds

Section 16. Highway Bonds

Article X: County and Municipal Corporations – Page 101

Section 1. Salaries and Fees of County Officers

Section 2. Terms of County Officers

Section 3. Removal of County Seat

Section 4. Combined City and County Municipal Corporations

Section 5. Incorporated Counties

Section 6. Municipal Elections; Charters; Legislative Powers and Taxation

Section 7. Five-Member Board of County Commissioners

Section 8. Services Mandated by State Rule or Regulation

Section 9. Recall of Elected County Official

Section 10. Urban Counties; Powers and Functions; Charters

Section 11. Single Urban Government

Article XI: Corporations
Other Than Municipal – Page 113

Section 1. Public Regulation Commission; Creation, Membership, Terms, Qualifications

Section 2. Public Regulation Commission Responsibilities

Section 13. Laws Relating to Corporations

Section 14. Supremacy of Police Power

Section 18. Eminent Domain

Section 19. Chartering Corporations

Section 20. Creation of Office Of Superintendent of Insurance

Article XII: Education – Page 116

Section 1. Public Schools

Section 2. Permanent School Fund

Section 3. Private School Funding

Section 4. Current School Fund

Section 5. Mandatory School Attendance

Section 6. Public Education Department; Public Education Commission

Section 7. Permanent School Fund Investments

Section 8. Teacher Training in Languages

Section 9. Religious Tests and Services

Section 10. Children of Spanish Descent

Section 11. State Educational Institutions

Section 12. Land Granted by Enabling Act

Section 13. Board of Regents

Section 14. Recall of School Board Member

Section 15. Seven-Member School Boards

Article XIII: Public Lands – Page 126

Section 1. Declaration and Purpose

Section 2. Commissioner of Public Lands

Section 3. Patents

Article XIV: Public Institutions – Page 128

Section 1. State Institutions

Section 2. Purpose of Granted Land

Section 3. Control and Management

Article XV: Agriculture and Conservation – Page 129

Section 1. Department of Agriculture

Section 2. Police Power Extended to Forest Lands

Article XVI: Irrigation and Water Rights – Page 130

Section 1. Rights to Use Waters

Section 2. Public Waters Subject to Appropriation

Section 3. Beneficial Use

Section 4. Drainage Districts and Systems

Section 5. Appeals Relating to Water Rights

Section 6. Water Trust Fund

Article XVII: Mines and Mining – Page 132

Section 1. State Mine Inspector

Section 2. Mine Safety; Employment of Children

Article XVIII: Militia – Page 133

Section 1. Composition of State Militia

Section 2. Organization, Discipline, and Equipment of the Militia

Article XIX: Amendments – Page 134

Section 1. Proposal and Publication; Voting and Ratification

Section 2. Constitutional Convention

Section 3. Laws Enacted by Direct Vote

Section 4. Amendments of Compact with United States

Article XX: Miscellaneous – Page 137

Section 1. Oath of Office

Section 2. Succession of Officers

Section 3. Commencement of Term of Office

Section 4. Vacancy in Office of District Attorney or County Commissioner

Section 5. Vacancy of Appointed Officers

Section 6. General Election Date

Section 7. County Canvassing

Section 8. Elections Upon State Admission

Section 9. Officer's Compensation

Section 10. Employment of Children

Section 11. Women as Public Officers

Section 12. Publication of Laws in English and Spanish

Section 13. Wines for Sacramental Purposes

Section 14. Railroad Transportation of Public Officials

Section 15. Penitentiary Inmates; Employment and Earnings

Section 16. Liability of Railroads to Employees

Section 18. Leasing of Convict Labor

Section 19. Government Work-Day

Section 20. Waiver of Indictment

Section 21. Protection of the Environment

Section 22. Public Employees and Educational Retirement Systems Trust Funds

Article XXI: Compact With The United States – Page 144

Preamble

Section 1. Freedom of Religion; Polygamous Marriages

Section 2. Lands Owned by Indian Tribes or the United States; Taxation

Section 3. Indebtedness Prior to Statehood

Section 4. Public Schools; Sectarian Control; English Language

Section 5. Right to Vote

Section 6. State Capital

Section 7. Irrigation Works

Section 8. Disposal of Lands Within Indian Reservations; Liquor Laws

Section 9. Lands Granted to State Subject To Enabling Act

Section 10. Revocation or Amendment

Section 11. Valuation and Exchange of Lands

Article XXII: Schedule – Page 148

Section 1. Effective Date

Section 2. Continuing Effect of Act Relating to Liability of Common Carriers

Section 3. Continuing Effect of the Act for the Protection of Miners

Section 4. Continuing Effect of Territorial Laws

Section 5. Pardoning Power

Section 6. Territorial Property

Section 7. Territorial Obligations and Undertakings

Section 8. Territorial Court Proceedings and Judgments

Section 9. Territorial Courts, Offices, and Appointments; Seals

Section 10. Pending Territorial Court Proceedings

Section 11. Signing of Constitution

Section 12. Counties, Municipalities, and Districts; Debts, Names, and Boundaries

Section 13. Ratification of Constitution by Election

Section 14. Constitution Ballots

Section 15. Constitution Canvassing Board

Section 16. Approval of Constitution by President and Congress

Section 17. First Election of Officers

Section 18. Canvassing and Certification of Election

Section 19. Assumption of Office

Section 20. Convening of the Legislature

Section 21. Laws to Effectuate the Constitution

Section 22. Term of Elected Officers

Article XXIII: Intoxicating Liquors – Page 155

Repealed.

Article XXIV: Leases on State Land – Page 156

Section 1. Royalty Leases and Contracts

Preamble

We, the people of New Mexico, grateful to Almighty God for the blessings of liberty, in order to secure the advantages of a state government, do ordain and establish this constitution.

ARTICLE I: NAME AND BOUNDARIES

Section 1. Name and Boundaries

The name of this state is New Mexico, and its boundaries are as follows:

Beginning at the point where the thirty-seventh parallel of north latitude intersects the one hundred and third meridian west from Greenwich; thence along said one hundred and third meridian to the thirty-second parallel of north latitude; thence along said thirty-second parallel to the Rio Grande, also known as the Rio Bravo del Norte, as it existed on the ninth day of September, one thousand eight hundred and fifty; thence, following the main channel of said river, as it existed on the ninth day of September, one thousand eight hundred and fifty, to the parallel of thirty-one degrees forty-seven minutes north latitude; thence west one hundred miles to a point; thence south to the parallel of thirty-one degrees twenty minutes north latitude; thence along said parallel of thirty-one degrees twenty minutes, to the thirty-second meridian of longitude west from Washington; thence along said thirty-second meridian to the thirty-seventh parallel of north latitude; thence along said thirty-seventh parallel to the point of beginning.

ARTICLE II: BILL OF RIGHTS

Section 1. Supreme Law of the Land

The state of New Mexico is an inseparable part of the federal union, and the constitution of the United States is the supreme law of the land.

Section 2. Popular Sovereignty

All political power is vested in and derived from the people: all government of right originates with the people, is founded upon their will and is instituted solely for their good.

Section 3. Right of Self-Government

The people of the state have the sole and exclusive right to govern themselves as a free, sovereign and independent state.

Section 4. Inherent Rights

All persons are born equally free, and have certain natural, inherent and inalienable rights, among which are the rights of enjoying and defending life and liberty, of acquiring, possessing and protecting property, and of seeking and obtaining safety and happiness.

Section 5. Rights under Treaty of Guadalupe Hidalgo Preserved

The rights, privileges and immunities, civil, political and religious guaranteed to the people of New Mexico by the Treaty of Guadalupe Hidalgo shall be preserved inviolate.

Section 6. Right to Bear Arms

No law shall abridge the right of the citizen to keep and bear arms for security and defense, for lawful hunting and recreational use and for other lawful purposes, but nothing herein shall be held to permit the carrying of concealed weapons. No municipality or county shall regulate, in any way, an incident of the right to keep and bear arms.

Section 7. Habeas Corpus

The privilege of the writ of habeas corpus shall never be suspended, unless, in case of rebellion or invasion, the public safety requires it.

Section 8. Freedom of Elections

All elections shall be free and open, and no power, civil or military, shall at any time interfere to prevent the free exercise of the right of suffrage.

Section 9. Military Power Subordinate; Quartering of Soldiers

The military shall always be in strict subordination to the civil power; no soldier shall in time of peace be quartered in any house without the consent of the owner, nor in time of war except in the manner prescribed by law.

Section 10. Searches and Seizures

The people shall be secure in their persons, papers, homes and effects, from unreasonable searches and seizures, and no warrant to search any place, or seize any person or thing, shall issue without describing the place to be searched, or the persons or things to be seized, nor without a written showing of probable cause, supported by oath or affirmation.

Section 11. Freedom of Religion

Every man shall be free to worship God according to the dictates of his own conscience, and no person shall ever be molested or denied any civil or political right or privilege on account of his religious opinion or mode of religious worship. No person shall be required to attend any place of worship or support any religious sect or denomination; nor shall any preference be given by law to any religious denomination or mode of worship.

Section 12. Trial by Jury; Less Than Unanimous Verdicts in Civil Cases

The right of trial by jury as it has heretofore existed shall be secured to all and remain inviolate. In all cases triable in courts inferior to the district court the jury may consist of six. The legislature may provide that verdicts in civil cases may be rendered by less than a unanimous vote of the jury.

Section 13. Bail; Excessive Fines; Cruel and Unusual Punishment

All persons shall, before conviction, be bailable by sufficient sureties, except for capital offenses when the proof is evident or the presumption great and in situations in which bail is specifically prohibited by this section. Excessive bail shall not be required, nor excessive fines imposed, nor cruel and unusual punishment inflicted.

Bail may be denied by a court of record pending trial for a defendant charged with a felony if the prosecuting authority requests a hearing and proves by clear and convincing evidence that no release conditions will reasonably protect the safety of any other person or the community. An appeal from an order denying bail shall be given preference over all other matters. A person who is not a danger detainable on grounds of dangerousness nor a flight risk in the absence of bond and is otherwise eligible for bail shall not be detained solely because of financial inability to post a money or property bond. A defendant who is neither a danger nor a flight risk and who has a financial inability to post a money or property bond may file a motion with the court requesting relief from the requirement to post bond. The court shall rule on the motion in an expedited manner.

Section 14. Indictment and Information; Grand Juries; Rights of Accused

No person shall be held to answer for a capital, felonious or infamous crime unless on a presentment or indictment of a grand jury or information filed by a district attorney or attorney general or their deputies, except in cases arising in the militia when in actual service in time of war or public danger. No person shall be so held on information without having had a preliminary examination before an examining magistrate, or having waived such preliminary examination.

A grand jury shall be composed of such number, not less than twelve, as may be prescribed by law. Citizens only, residing in the county for which a grand jury may be convened and qualified as prescribed by law, may serve on a grand jury. Concurrence necessary for the finding of an indictment by a grand jury shall be prescribed by law; provided, such concurrence shall never be by less than a majority of those who compose a grand jury, and, provided, at least eight must concur in finding an indictment when a grand jury is composed of twelve in number. Until otherwise prescribed by law a grand jury shall be composed of twelve in number of which eight must concur in finding an indictment. A grand jury shall be convened upon order of a judge of a court empowered to try and determine cases of capital, felonious or infamous crimes at such times as to him shall be deemed necessary, or a grand jury shall be ordered to convene by such judge upon the filing of a petition therefore signed by not less than the greater of two hundred registered voters or two percent of the registered voters of the county, or a grand jury may be convened in any additional manner as may be prescribed by law.

In all criminal prosecutions, the accused shall have the right to appear and defend himself in person, and by counsel; to demand the nature and cause of the accusation; to be confronted with the witnesses against him; to have the charge and testimony interpreted to him in a language that he understands; to have compulsory process to compel the attendance of necessary witnesses in his behalf, and a speedy public trial by an impartial jury of the county or district in which the offense is alleged to have been committed.

Section 15. Self-Incrimination; Double Jeopardy

No person shall be compelled to testify against himself in a criminal proceeding, nor shall any person be twice put in jeopardy for the same offense; and when the indictment, information or affidavit upon which any person is convicted charges different offenses or different degrees of the same offense and a new trial is granted the accused, he may not again be tried for an offense or degree of the offense greater than the one of which he was convicted.

Section 16. Treason

Treason against the state shall consist only in levying war against it, adhering to its enemies, or giving them aid and comfort. No person shall be convicted of treason unless on the testimony of two witnesses to the same overt act, or on confession in open court.

Section 17. Freedom of Speech and Press; Libel

Every person may freely speak, write and publish his sentiments on all subjects, being responsible for the abuse of that right; and no law shall be passed to restrain or abridge the liberty of speech or of the press. In all criminal prosecutions for libels, the truth may be given in evidence to the jury; and if it shall appear to the jury that the matter charged as libelous is true and was published with good motives and for justifiable ends, the party shall be acquitted.

Section 18. Due Process; Equal Protection; Sex Discrimination

No person shall be deprived of life, liberty or property without due process of law; nor shall any person be denied equal protection of the laws. Equality of rights under law shall not be denied on account of the sex of any person.

Section 19. Retroactive Laws; Bills of Attainder; Impairment of Contracts

No ex post facto law, bill of attainder nor law impairing the obligation of contracts shall be enacted by the legislature.

Section 20. Eminent Domain

Private property shall not be taken or damaged for public use without just compensation.

Section 21. Imprisonment for Debt

No person shall be imprisoned for debt in any civil action.

Section 22. Alien Landownership

Repealed.

Section 23. Reserved Rights

The enumeration in this constitution of certain rights shall not be construed to deny, impair or disparage others retained by the people.

Section 24. Victim's Rights

A. A victim of arson resulting in bodily injury, aggravated arson, aggravated assault, aggravated battery, dangerous use of explosives, negligent use of a deadly weapon, murder, voluntary manslaughter, involuntary manslaughter, kidnapping, criminal sexual penetration, criminal sexual contact of a minor, homicide by vehicle, great bodily injury by vehicle or abandonment or abuse of a child or that victim's representative shall have the following rights as provided by law:

(1) the right to be treated with fairness and respect for the victim's dignity and privacy throughout the criminal justice process;

(2) the right to timely disposition of the case;

(3) the right to be reasonably protected from the accused throughout the criminal justice process;

(4) the right to notification of court proceedings;

(5) the right to attend all public court proceedings the accused has the right to attend;

(6) the right to confer with the prosecution;

(7) the right to make a statement to the court at sentencing and at any post-sentencing hearings for the accused;

(8) the right to restitution from the person convicted of the criminal conduct that caused the victim's loss or injury;

(9) the right to information about the conviction, sentencing, imprisonment, escape or release of the accused;

(10) the right to have the prosecuting attorney notify the victim's employer, if requested by the victim, of the necessity of the victim's cooperation and testimony in a court proceeding that may necessitate the absence of the victim from work for good cause; and

(11) the right to promptly receive any property belonging to the victim that is being held for evidentiary purposes by a law enforcement agency or the prosecuting attorney, unless there are compelling evidentiary reasons for retention of the victim's property.

B. A person accused or convicted of a crime against a victim shall have no standing to object to any failure by any person to comply with the provisions of Subsection A of Section 24 of Article 2 of the constitution of New Mexico.

C. The provisions of this amendment shall not take effect until the legislature enacts laws to implement this amendment.

ARTICLE III: DISTRIBUTION OF POWER

Section 1. Separation of Departments; Establishment of Workers Compensation Body

The powers of the government of this state are divided into three distinct departments, the legislative, executive and judicial, and no person or collection of persons charged with the exercise of powers properly belonging to one of these departments, shall exercise any powers properly belonging to either of the others, except as in this constitution otherwise expressly directed or permitted. Nothing in this section, or elsewhere in this constitution, shall prevent the legislature from establishing, by statute, a body with statewide jurisdiction other than the courts of this state for the determination of rights and liabilities between persons when those rights and liabilities arise from transactions or occurrences involving personal injury sustained in the course of employment by an employee. The statute shall provide for the type and organization of the body, the mode of appointment or election of its members and such other matters as the legislature may deem necessary or proper.

ARTICLE IV: LEGISLATIVE DEPARTMENT

Section 1. Vesting of Legislative Power; Location of Sessions; Referendum on Legislation

The legislative power shall be vested in a senate and house of representatives which shall be designated the legislature of the state of New Mexico, and shall hold its sessions at the seat of government.

The people reserve the power to disapprove, suspend and annul any law enacted by the legislature, except general appropriation laws; laws providing for the preservation of the public peace, health or safety; for the payment of the public debt or interest thereon, or the creation or funding of the same, except as in this constitution otherwise provided; for the maintenance of the public schools or state institutions, and local or special laws. Petitions disapproving any law other than those above excepted, enacted at the last preceding session of the legislature, shall be filed with the secretary of state not less than four months prior to the next general election. Such petitions shall be signed by not less than ten per centum of the qualified electors of each of three-fourths of the counties and in the aggregate by not less than ten per centum of the qualified electors of the state, as shown by the total number of votes cast at the last preceding general election. The question of the approval or rejection of such law shall be submitted by the secretary of state to the electorate at the next general election; and if a majority of the legal votes cast thereon, and not less than forty per centum of the total number of legal votes cast at such general election, be cast for the rejection of such law, it shall be annulled and thereby repealed with the same effect as if the legislature had then repealed it, and such repeal shall revive any law repealed by the act so annulled; otherwise, it shall remain in force unless subsequently repealed by the legislature. If such petition or petitions be signed by not less than twenty-five per centum of the qualified electors under each of the foregoing conditions, and be filed with the secretary of state within ninety days after the adjournment of the session of the legislature at which such law was enacted, the operation thereof shall be thereupon suspended and the question of its approval or rejection shall be likewise submitted to a vote at the next ensuing general election. If a majority of the votes cast thereon and not less than forty per centum of the total number of votes cast at such general election be cast for its rejection, it shall be thereby annulled; otherwise, it shall go into effect upon publication of the certificate of the secretary of state declaring the result of the vote thereon. It shall be a felony for any person to sign any such petition with any name other than his own, or to sign his name more than once for the same measure, or to sign such petition when he is not a qualified elector in the county specified in such petition; provided, that nothing herein shall be construed to prohibit the writing thereon of the name of any person who cannot write, and who signs the same with his mark. The legislature shall enact laws necessary for the effective exercise of the power hereby reserved.

Section 2. Powers Generally; Disaster Emergency Procedure

In addition to the powers herein enumerated, the legislature shall have all powers necessary to the legislature of a free state, including the power to enact reasonable and appropriate laws to guarantee the continuity and effective operation of state and local government by providing emergency procedure for use only during periods of disaster emergency. A disaster emergency is defined as a period when damage or injury to persons or property in this state, caused by enemy attack, is of such magnitude that a state of martial law is declared to exist in the state, and a disaster emergency is declared by the chief executive officer of the United States and the chief executive officer of this state, and the legislature has not declared by joint resolution that the disaster emergency is ended. Upon the declaration of a disaster emergency the chief executive of the state shall within seven days call a special session of the legislature which shall remain in continuous session during the disaster emergency, and may recess from time to time for [not] more than three days.

Section 3. Number and Qualifications of Members; Single-Member Districts; Reapportionment

A. Senators shall not be less than twenty-five years of age and representatives not less than twenty-one years of age at the time of their election. If any senator or representative permanently removes his residence from or maintains no residence in the district from which he was elected, then he shall be deemed to have resigned and his successor shall be selected as provided in Section 4 of this article. No person shall be eligible to serve in the legislature who, at the time of qualifying, holds any office of trust or profit with the state, county or national governments, except notaries public and officers of the militia who receive no salary.

B. The senate shall be composed of no more than forty-two members elected from single-member districts.

C. The house of representatives shall be composed of no more than seventy members elected from single-member districts.

D. Once following publication of the official report of each federal decennial census hereafter conducted, the legislature may by statute reapportion its membership.

Section 4. Terms of Office of Members; Time of Election; Filling of Vacancies

Members of the legislature shall be elected as follows: those senators from Bernalillo, Chaves, Curry, DeBaca, Grant, Lea, Lincoln, Luna, Sandoval, San Juan, San Miguel, Socorro, Taos, Torrance, Union and Valencia counties for a term of six years starting January 1, 1961, and after serving such terms shall be elected for a term of four years thereafter; those senators from all other counties for the terms of four years, and members of the house of representatives for a term of two years. They shall be elected on the day provided by law for holding the general election of state officers or representatives in congress. If a vacancy occurs in the office of senator or member of the house of representatives, for any reason, the county commissioners of the county wherein the vacancy occurs shall fill such vacancy by appointment.

Such legislative appointments as provided in this section shall be for a term ending on December 31, subsequent to the next succeeding general election.

Section 5. Time and Length of Sessions; Items Considered in Even-Numbered Years

A. Each regular session of the legislature shall begin annually at 12:00 noon on the third Tuesday of January. Every regular session of the legislature convening during an odd-numbered year shall remain in session not to exceed sixty days, and every regular session of the legislature convening during an even-numbered year shall remain in session not to exceed thirty days. No special session of the legislature shall exceed thirty days.
B. Every regular session of the legislature convening during an even-numbered year shall consider only the following:

(1) budgets, appropriations and revenue bills;

(2) bills drawn pursuant to special messages of the governor; and

(3) bills of the last previous regular session vetoed by the governor.

Section 6. Special Session; Extraordinary Session

Special sessions of the legislature may be called by the governor, but no business shall be transacted except such as relates to the objects specified in this proclamation. Provided, however, that when three-fifths of the members elected to the house of representatives and three-fifths of the members elected to the senate shall have certified to the governor of the state of New Mexico that in their opinion an emergency exists in the affairs of the state of New Mexico, it shall thereupon be the duty of said governor and mandatory upon him, within five days from the receipt of such certificate or certificates, to convene said legislature in extraordinary session for all purposes; and in the event said governor shall, within said time, Sundays excluded, fail or refuse to convene said legislature as aforesaid, then and in that event said legislature may convene itself in extraordinary session, as if convened in regular session, for all purposes, provided that such extraordinary self-convened session shall be limited to a period of thirty days, unless at the expiration of said period, there shall be pending an impeachment trial of some officer of the state government, in which event the legislature shall be authorized to remain in session until such trial shall have been completed.

Section 7. Judge of Election and Qualification of Members; Quorum

Each house shall be the judge of the election and qualifications of its own members. A majority of either house shall constitute a quorum to do business, but a less number may effect a temporary organization, adjourn from day to day and compel the attendance of absent members.

Section 8. Call to Order; Presiding Officers

The senate shall be called to order in the hall of the senate by the lieutenant governor. The senate shall elect a president pro tempore who shall preside in the absence of the lieutenant governor and shall serve until the next session of the legislature. The house of representatives shall be called to order in the hall of said house by the secretary of state. He shall preside until the election of a speaker, who shall be the member receiving the highest number of votes for that office.

Section 9. Selection and Compensation of Officers and Employees

The legislature shall select its own officers and employees and fix their compensation. Each house shall have one chaplain, one chief clerk and one sergeant at arms; and there shall be one assistant chief clerk and one assistant sergeant at arms for each house; and each house may employ such enrolling clerks, reading clerks, stenographers, janitors and such subordinate employees in addition to those enumerated, as they may reasonably require and their compensation shall be fixed by the said legislature at the beginning of each session.

Section 10. Compensation of Members

Each member of the legislature shall receive:

A. per diem at the internal revenue service per diem rate for the city of Santa Fe for each day's attendance during each session of the legislature and the internal revenue service standard mileage rate for each mile traveled in going to and returning from the seat of government by the usual traveled route, once each session as defined by Article 4, Section 5 of this constitution;

B. per diem expense and mileage at the same rates as provided in Subsection A of this section for service at meetings required by legislative committees established by the legislature to meet in the interim between sessions; and

C. no other compensation, perquisite or allowance.

Section 11. Rules of Procedure; Contempt or Disorderly Conduct; Expulsion of Members

Each house may determine the rules of its procedure, punish its members or others for contempt or disorderly behavior in its presence and protect its members against violence; and may, with the concurrence of two-thirds of its members, expel a member, but not a second time for the same act. Punishment for contempt or disorderly behavior or by expulsion shall not be a bar to criminal prosecution.

Section 12. Public Sessions; Journals

All sessions of each house shall be public. Each house shall keep a journal of its proceedings and the yeas and nays on any questions shall, at the request of one-fifth of the members present, be entered thereon. The original thereof shall be filed with the secretary of state at the close of the session, and shall be printed and published under his authority.

Section 13. Privileges and Immunities

Members of the legislature shall, in all cases except treason, felony and breach of the peace, be privileged from arrest during their attendance at the sessions of their respective houses, and on going to and returning from the same. And they shall not be questioned in any other place for any speech or debate or for any vote cast in either house.

Section 14. Adjournment

Neither house shall, without the consent of the other, adjourn for more than three days, Sundays excepted; nor to any other place than that where the two houses are sitting; and on the day of the final adjournment they shall adjourn at twelve o'clock, noon.

Section 15. Laws to Be Passed by Bill; Alteration of Bill; Enacting Clause; Printing and Reading of Bill

No law shall be passed except by bill, and no bill shall be so altered or amended on its passage through either house as to change its original purpose. The enacting clause of all bills shall be: "Be it enacted by the legislature of the state of New Mexico." Any bill may originate in either house. No bill, except bills to provide for the public peace, health and safety, and the codification or revision of the laws, shall become a law unless it has been printed, and read three different times in each house, not more than two of which readings shall be on the same day, and the third of which shall be in full.

Section 16. Subject of Bill in Title; Appropriation Bills

The subject of every bill shall be clearly expressed in its title, and no bill embracing more than one subject shall be passed except general appropriation bills and bills for the codification or revision of the laws; but if any subject is embraced in any act which is not expressed in its title, only so much of the act as is not so expressed shall be void. General appropriation bills shall embrace nothing but appropriations for the expense of the executive, legislative and judiciary departments, interest, sinking fund, payments on the public debt, public schools and other expenses required by existing laws; but if any such bill contain any other matter, only so much thereof as is hereby forbidden to be placed therein shall be void. All other appropriations shall be made by separate bills.

Section 17. Passage of Bills

No bill shall be passed except by a vote of a majority of the members present in each house, nor unless on its final passage a vote be taken by yeas and nays, and entered on the journal.

Section 18. Amendment of Statutes

No law shall be revised or amended, or the provisions thereof extended by reference to its title only; but each section thereof as revised, amended or extended shall be set out in full. Notwithstanding the foregoing or any other provision of this constitution, the legislature, in any law imposing a tax or taxes, may define the amount on, in respect to or by which such tax or taxes are imposed or measured, by reference to any provision of the laws of the United States as the same may be or become effective at any time or from time to time, and may prescribe exceptions or modifications to any such provision.

Section 19. Introduction of Bills

Time limitation on the introduction of bills at any session of the legislature shall be established by law.

Section 20. Enrollment, Engrossment and Signing of Bills

Immediately after the passage of any bill or resolution, it shall be enrolled and engrossed, and read publicly in full in each house, and thereupon shall be signed by the presiding officers of each house in open session, and the fact of such reading and signing shall be entered on the journal. No interlineation or erasure in a signed bill, shall be effective, unless certified thereon in express terms by the presiding officer of each house quoting the words interlined or erased, nor unless the fact of the making of such interlineation or erasure be publicly announced in each house and entered on the journal.

Section 21. Alteration or Theft of Bill

Any person who shall, without lawful authority, materially change or alter, or make away with, any bill pending in or passed by the legislature, shall be deemed guilty of a felony and upon conviction thereof shall be punished by imprisonment in the penitentiary for not less than one year nor more than five years.

Section 22. Governor's Approval or Veto of Bills

Every bill passed by the legislature shall, before it becomes a law, be presented to the governor for approval. If he approves, he shall sign it, and deposit it with the secretary of state; otherwise, he shall return it to the house in which it originated, with his objections, which shall be entered at large upon the journal; and such bill shall not become a law unless thereafter approved by two-thirds of the members present and voting in each house by yea and nay vote entered upon its journal. Any bill not returned by the governor within three days, Sundays excepted, after being presented to him, shall become a law, whether signed by him or not, unless the legislature by adjournment prevent such return. Every bill presented to the governor during the last three days of the session shall be approved by him within twenty days after the adjournment and shall be by him immediately deposited with the secretary of state. Unless so approved and signed by him such bill shall not become a law. The governor may in like manner approve or disapprove any part or parts, item or items, of any bill appropriating money, and such parts or items approved shall become a law, and such as are disapproved shall be void unless passed over his veto, as herein provided.

Section 23. Effective Date of Law; Emergency Acts

Laws shall go into effect ninety days after the adjournment of the legislature enacting them, except general appropriation laws, which shall go into effect immediately upon their passage and approval. Any act necessary for the preservation of the public peace, health or safety, shall take effect immediately upon its passage and approval, provided it be passed by two-thirds vote of each house and such necessity be stated in a separate section.

Section 24. Local or Special Laws

The legislature shall not pass local or special laws in any of the following cases: regulating county, precinct or district affairs; the jurisdiction and duties of justices of the peace, police magistrates and constables; the practice in courts of justice; the rate of interest on money; the punishment for crimes and misdemeanors; the assessment or collection of taxes or extending the time of collection thereof; the summoning and impaneling of jurors; the management of public schools; the sale or mortgaging of real estate of minors or others under disability; the change of venue in civil or criminal cases. Nor in the following cases: granting divorces; laying out, opening, altering or working roads or highways, except as to state roads extending into more than one county, and military roads; vacating roads, town plats, streets, alleys or public grounds; locating or changing county seats, or changing county lines, except in creating new counties; incorporating cities, towns or villages, or changing or amending the charter of any city, town or village; the opening or conducting of any election or designating the place of voting; declaring any person of age; chartering or licensing ferries, toll bridges, toll roads, banks, insurance companies or loan and trust companies; remitting fines, penalties, forfeitures or taxes; or refunding money paid into the state treasury, or relinquishing, extending or extinguishing, in whole or in part, any indebtedness or liability of any person or corporation, to the state or any municipality therein; creating, increasing or decreasing fees, percentages or allowances of public officers; changing the laws of descent; granting to any corporation, association or individual the right to lay down railroad tracks or any special or exclusive privilege, immunity or franchise, or amending existing charters for such purpose; changing the rules of evidence in any trial or inquiry; the limitation of actions; giving effect to any informal or invalid deed, will or other instrument; exempting property from taxation; restoring to citizenship any person convicted of an infamous crime; the adoption or legitimizing of children; changing the name of persons or places; and the creation, extension or impairment of liens. In every other case where a general law can be made applicable, no special law shall be enacted.

Section 25. Validating Unauthorized Official Acts; Fines Against Officers, Etc

No law shall be enacted legalizing the unauthorized or invalid act of any officer, remitting any fine, penalty or judgment against any officer or validating any illegal use of public funds.

Section 26. Grant of Franchise or Privilege

The legislature shall not grant to any corporation or person, any rights, franchises, privileges, immunities or exemptions, which shall not, upon the same terms and under like conditions, inure equally to all persons or corporations; no exclusive right, franchise, privilege or immunity shall be granted by the legislature or any municipality in this state.

Section 27. Extra or Increased Compensation for Officers, Contractors, Etc

No law shall be enacted giving any extra compensation to any public officer, servant, agent or contractor after services are rendered or contract made; nor shall the compensation of any officer be increased or diminished during his term of office, except as otherwise provided in this constitution.

Section 28. Appointment of Present and Former Legislators to Office; Interest of Legislators in Contracts

No member of the legislature shall, during the term for which he was elected, be appointed to any civil office in the state, nor shall he within one year thereafter be appointed to any civil office created, or the emoluments of which were increased during such term; nor shall any member of the legislature during the term for which he was elected nor within one year thereafter, be interested directly or indirectly in any contract with the state or any municipality thereof, which was authorized by any law passed during such term.

Section 29. Laws Creating Debts

No law authorizing indebtedness shall be enacted which does not provide for levying a tax sufficient to pay the interest, and for the payment at maturity of the principal.

Section 30. Payments from Treasury to Be Upon Appropriations and Warrant

Except interest or other payments on the public debt, money shall be paid out of the treasury only upon appropriations made by the legislature. No money shall be paid therefrom except upon warrant drawn by the proper officer. Every law making an appropriation shall distinctly specify the sum appropriated and the object to which it is to be applied.

Section 31. Appropriations for Charitable, Educational, Etc., Purposes

No appropriation shall be made for charitable, educational or other benevolent purposes to any person, corporation, association, institution or community, not under the absolute control of the state, but the legislature may, in its discretion, make appropriations for the charitable institutions and hospitals, for the maintenance of which annual appropriations were made by the legislative assembly of nineteen hundred and nine.

Section 32. Remission of Debts Due State or Municipalities

No obligation or liability of any person, association or corporation held or owned by or owing to the state, or any municipal corporation therein, shall ever be exchanged, transferred, remitted, released, postponed or in any way diminished by the legislature, nor shall any such obligation or liability be extinguished except by the payment thereof into the proper treasury, or by proper proceeding in court. Provided that the obligations created by Special Session Laws 1955, Chapter 5, running to the state or any of its agencies, remaining unpaid on the effective date of this amendment are void.

Section 33. Prosecutions under Repealed Laws

No person shall be exempt from prosecution and punishment for any crime or offenses against any law of this state by reason of the subsequent repeal of such law.

Section 34. Change of Rights or Procedure in Pending Cases

No act of the legislature shall affect the right or remedy of either party, or change the rules of evidence or procedure, in any pending case.

Section 35. Power and Procedure for Impeachment and Trial

The sole power of impeachment shall be vested in the house of representatives, and a concurrence of a majority of all the members elected shall be necessary to the proper exercise thereof. All impeachments shall be tried by the senate. When sitting for that purpose the senators shall be under oath or affirmation to do justice according to the law and the evidence. When the governor or lieutenant governor is on trial, the chief justice of the supreme court shall preside. No person shall be convicted without the concurrence of two-thirds of the senators elected.

Section 36. Officers Subject to Impeachment

All state officers and judges of the district court shall be liable to impeachment for crimes, misdemeanors and malfeasance in office, but judgment in such cases shall not extend further than removal from office and disqualification to hold any office of honor, trust or profit, or to vote under the laws of this state; but such officer or judge, whether convicted or acquitted shall, nevertheless, be liable to prosecution, trial, judgment, punishment or civil action, according to law. No officer shall exercise any powers or duties of his office after notice of his impeachment is served upon him until he is acquitted.

Section 37. Railroad Passes

It shall not be lawful for a member of the legislature to use a pass, or to purchase or receive transportation over any railroad upon terms not open to the general public; and the violation of this section shall work a forfeiture of the office.

Section 38. Monopolies

The legislature shall enact laws to prevent trusts, monopolies and combinations in restraint of trade.

Section 39. "Bribery" and "solicitation" Defined

Any member of the legislature who shall vote or use his influence for or against any matter pending in either house in consideration of any money, thing of value or promise thereof, shall be deemed guilty of bribery; and any member of the legislature or other person who shall directly or indirectly offer, give or promise any money, thing of value, privilege or personal advantage, to any member of the legislature to influence him to vote or work for or against any matter pending in either house; or any member of the legislature who shall solicit from any person or corporation any money, thing of value or personal advantage for his vote or influence as such member shall be deemed guilty of solicitation of bribery.

Section 40. Penalty for Bribery

Any person convicted of any of the offenses mentioned in Sections thirty-seven and thirty-nine hereof, shall be deemed guilty of a felony and upon conviction shall be punished by fine of not more than one thousand dollars [($1,000)] or by imprisonment in the penitentiary for not less than one nor more than five years.

Section 41. Compelling Testimony in Bribery Cases

Any person may be compelled to testify in any lawful investigation or judicial proceeding against another charged with bribery or solicitation of bribery as defined herein, and shall not be permitted to withhold his testimony on the ground that it might incriminate or subject him to public infamy; but such testimony shall not be used against him in any judicial proceeding against him except for perjury in giving such testimony.

Section 42. Hearings on Confirmation of Gubernatorial Appointments

The senate, in exercising its advice and consent responsibilities over gubernatorial appointments, may by resolution designate the members of an appropriate standing committee to operate as an interim committee during the interim between legislative sessions for the purpose of conducting hearings and taking testimony on the confirmation or rejection of gubernatorial appointments. Recommendations of the committee shall be submitted to the senate for action at the next succeeding legislative session. Members of such committee shall be paid per diem and mileage for attendance at such hearings at the same rates as legislators are paid for attendance at joint legislative interim committee meetings. The governor shall submit all appointments requiring senate confirmation to such committee within thirty days after the date of appointment.

ARTICLE V: EXECUTIVE DEPARTMENT

Section 1. Composition of Department; Terms of Office of Members; Residing and Maintaining Records at Seat of Government

The executive department shall consist of a governor, lieutenant governor, secretary of state, state auditor, state treasurer, attorney general and commissioner of public lands, who shall, unless otherwise provided in the constitution of New Mexico, be elected for terms of four years beginning on the first day of January next after their election. The governor and lieutenant governor shall be elected jointly by the casting by each voter of a single vote applicable to both offices.
Such officers shall, after having served two terms in a state office, be ineligible to hold that state office until one full term has intervened.

The officers of the executive department, except the lieutenant governor, shall during their terms of office, reside and keep the public records, books, papers and seals of office at the seat of government.

Upon the adoption of this amendment by the people, the terms provided for in this section shall apply to those officers elected at the general election in 1990 and all state executive officers elected thereafter.

Section 2. Canvass of Elections; Tie Votes

The returns of every election for state officers shall be sealed up and transmitted to the secretary of state, who, with the governor and chief justice, shall constitute the state canvassing board which shall canvass and declare the result of the election. The joint candidates having the highest number of votes cast for governor and lieutenant governor and the person having the highest number of votes for any other office, as shown by said returns, shall be declared duly elected. If two or more have an equal, and the highest, number of votes for the same office or offices, one of them, or any two for whom joint votes were cast for governor and lieutenant governor respectively, shall be chosen therefore by the legislature on joint ballot.

Section 3. Qualifications of Executive Officers

No person shall be eligible to any office specified in Section One, hereof, unless he be a citizen of the United States, at least thirty years of age, nor unless he shall have resided continuously in New Mexico for five years next preceding his election; nor to the office of attorney general, unless he be a licensed attorney of the supreme court of New Mexico in good standing; nor to the office of superintendent of public instruction unless he be a trained and experienced educator.

Section 4. Governor's Executive Power; Commander of Militia

The supreme executive power of the state shall be vested in the governor, who shall take care that the laws be faithfully executed. He shall be commander in chief of the military forces of the state, except when they are called into the service of the United States. He shall have power to call out the militia to preserve the public peace, execute the laws, suppress insurrection and repel invasion.

Section 5. Governor's Appointive and Removal Power; Interim Appointees

The governor shall nominate and, by and with the consent of the senate, appoint all officers whose appointment or election is not otherwise provided for and may remove any officer appointed by him unless otherwise provided by law. Should a vacancy occur in any state office, except lieutenant governor and member of the legislature, the governor shall fill such office by appointment, and such appointee shall hold office until the next general election, when his successor shall be chosen for the unexpired term.

Section 6. Governor's Power to Pardon and Reprieve

Subject to such regulations as may be prescribed by law, the governor shall have power to grant reprieves and pardons, after conviction for all offenses except treason and in cases of impeachment.

Section 7. Succession to Governorship

If at the time fixed for the beginning of the term of the governor, the governor-elect shall have died, the lieutenant governor-elect shall become governor. If a governor shall not have been chosen before the time fixed for the beginning of his term, or if the governor-elect shall have failed to qualify, then the lieutenant governor-elect shall act as governor until a governor shall have qualified; and the legislature may by law provide for the case wherein neither a governor-elect nor a lieutenant governor-elect shall have qualified, declaring who shall then act as governor, or the manner in which one who is to act shall be selected, and such person shall act accordingly until a governor or lieutenant governor shall have qualified.

If after the governor-elect has qualified a vacancy occurs in the office of governor, the lieutenant governor shall succeed to that office, and to all the powers, duties and emoluments thereof, provided he has by that time qualified for the office of lieutenant governor. In case the governor is absent from the state, or is for any reason unable to perform his duties, the lieutenant governor shall act as governor, with all the powers, duties and emoluments of that office until such disability be removed. In case there is no lieutenant governor, or in case he is for any reason unable to perform the duties of governor, then the secretary of state shall perform the duties of governor, and, in case there is no secretary of state, then the president pro tempore of the senate, or in case there is no president pro tempore of the senate, or he is for any reason unable to perform the duties of governor, then the speaker of the house shall succeed to the office of governor, or act as governor as hereinbefore provided.

Section 8. Lieutenant Governor to Be President of Senate

The lieutenant governor shall be president of the senate, but shall vote only when the senate is equally divided.

Section 9. Public Accounts and Reports

Each officer of the executive department and of the public institutions of the state shall keep an account of all moneys received by him and make reports thereof to the governor under oath, annually, and at such other times as the governor may require, and shall, at least thirty days preceding each regular session of the legislature, make a full and complete report to the governor, who shall transmit the same to the legislature.

Section 10. State Seal

There shall be a state seal which shall be called the "Great Seal of the State of New Mexico," and shall be kept by the secretary of state.

Section 11. Commissions

All commissions shall issue in the name of the state, be signed by the governor and attested by the secretary of state, who shall affix the state seal thereto.

Section 12. Compensation of Executive Officers

The annual compensation to be paid to the officers mentioned in Section One of this article shall be as follows: governor, five thousand dollars [($5,000)]; secretary of state, three thousand dollars [($3,000)]; state auditor, three thousand dollars [($3,000)]; state treasurer, three thousand dollars [($3,000)]; attorney general, four thousand dollars [($4,000)]; superintendent of public instruction, three thousand dollars [$3,000)]; and commissioner of public lands, three thousand dollars [($3,000)]; which compensation shall be paid to the

respective officers in equal quarterly payments.
The lieutenant governor shall receive ten dollars [($10.00)] per diem while acting as presiding officer of the senate, and mileage at the same rate as a state senator.

The compensation herein fixed shall be full payment for all services rendered by said officers and they shall receive no other fees or compensation whatsoever.

The compensation of any of said officers may be increased or decreased by law after the expiration of ten years from the date of the admission of New Mexico as a state.

Section 13. Residence of Public Officers; Election from Equal Districts

All district and municipal officers, county commissioners, school board members and municipal governing body members shall be residents of the political subdivision or district from which they are elected or for which they are appointed.

Counties, school districts and municipalities may be divided by their governing bodies into districts composed of populations as nearly equal as practicable for the purpose of electing the members of the respective governing bodies.

Section 14. State Transportation Commission

There is created a "state transportation commission."The members of the state transportation commission shall be appointed, shall have such power and shall perform such duties as may be provided by law. Notwithstanding the provisions of Article 5, Section 5 of the constitution of New Mexico, state transportation commissioners shall only be removed as provided by law.

Section 15. Confirmation of Cabinet Secretaries

The heads of all cabinet-level departments or agencies whose appointment is subject to confirmation by the senate shall be subject to confirmation or reconfirmation by the senate at the beginning of each term of a governor.

Section 15. Vacancy in the Office of the Lieutenant Governor

Whenever there is a vacancy in the office of the lieutenant governor, the governor shall nominate a lieutenant governor who shall take office upon confirmation by a majority vote of all members elected to the senate and shall serve the remainder of the unexpired term.

ARTICLE VI: JUDICIAL DEPARTMENT

Section 1. Judicial Power Vested

The judicial power of the state shall be vested in the senate when sitting as a court of impeachment, a supreme court, a court of appeals, district courts; probate courts, magistrate courts and such other courts inferior to the district courts as may be established by law from time to time in any district, county or municipality of the state.

Section 2. Supreme Court; Appellate Jurisdiction

Appeals from a judgment of the district court imposing a sentence of death or life imprisonment shall be taken directly to the supreme court. In all other cases, criminal and civil, the supreme court shall exercise appellate jurisdiction as may be provided by law; provided that an aggrieved party shall have an absolute right to one appeal.

Section 3. Supreme Court; Original Jurisdiction; Supervisory Control; Extraordinary Writs

The supreme court shall have original jurisdiction in quo warranto and mandamus against all state officers, boards and commissions, and shall have a superintending control over all inferior courts; it shall also have power to issue writs of mandamus, error, prohibition, habeas corpus, certiorari, injunction and all other writs necessary or proper for the complete exercise of its jurisdiction and to hear and determine the same. Such writs may be issued by direction of the court, or by any justice thereof. Each justice shall have power to issue writs of habeas corpus upon petition by or on behalf of a person held in actual custody, and to make such writs returnable before himself or before the supreme court, or before any of the district courts or any judge thereof.

Section 4. Supreme Court; Selection of Chief Justice

The supreme court of the state shall consist of at least five justices who shall be chosen as provided in this constitution. One of the justices shall be selected as chief justice as provided by law.

Section 5. Supreme Court; Quorum; Majority Concurring in Judgments

A majority of the justices of the supreme court shall be necessary to constitute a quorum for the transaction of business, and a majority of the justices must concur in any judgment of the court.

Section 6. Supreme Court; Absent or Disqualified Justice

When a justice of the supreme court shall be interested in any case, or be absent, or incapacitated, the remaining justices of the court may, in their discretion, call in any district judge of the state to act as a justice of the court.

Section 7. Supreme Court; Terms, Sessions and Recesses

The supreme court shall hold one term each year, commencing on the second Wednesday in January, and shall be at all times in session at the seat of government; provided, that the court may, from time to time, take such recess as in its judgment may be proper.

Section 8. Supreme Court; Qualifications of Justices

No person shall be qualified to hold the office of justice of the supreme court unless that person is at least thirty-five years old and has been in the actual practice of law for at least ten years preceding that person's assumption of office and has resided in this state for at least three years immediately preceding that person's assumption of office. The actual practice of law shall include a lawyer's service upon the bench of any court of this state. The increased qualifications provided by this 1988 amendment shall not apply to justices and judges serving at the time this amendment passes or elected at the general election in 1988.

Section 9. Supreme Court; Officers

The supreme court may appoint and remove at pleasure its reporter, bailiff, clerk and such other officers and assistants as may be prescribed by law.

Section 10. Supreme Court; Additional Justices

After the publication of the census of the United States in the year nineteen hundred and twenty, the legislature shall have power to increase the number of justices of the supreme court to five; provided, however, that no more than two of said justices shall be elected at one time, except to fill a vacancy.

Section 11. Supreme Court; Salary of Justices

The justices of the supreme court shall each receive such salary as may hereafter be fixed by law.

Section 12. Judicial Districts; District Judges

The state shall be divided into judicial districts as may be provided by law. One or more judges shall be chosen for each district as provided in this constitution.

Section 13. District Court; Jurisdiction and Terms

The district court shall have original jurisdiction in all matters and causes not excepted in this constitution, and such jurisdiction of special cases and proceedings as may be conferred by law, and appellate jurisdiction of all cases originating in inferior courts and tribunals in their respective districts, and supervisory control over the same. The district courts, or any judge thereof, shall have power to issue writs of habeas corpus, mandamus, injunction, quo warranto, certiorari, prohibition and all other writs, remedial or otherwise in the exercise of their jurisdiction; provided, that no such writs shall issue directed to judges or courts of equal or superior jurisdiction. The district courts shall also have the power of naturalization in accordance with the laws of the United States. Until otherwise provided by law, at least two terms of the district court shall be held annually in each county, at the county seat.

Section 14. District Court; Qualifications and Residence Requirement of Judges

The qualifications of the district judges shall be the same as those of justices of the supreme court except that district judges shall have been in the actual practice of law for at least six years preceding assumption of office. Each district judge shall reside in the district for which the judge was elected or appointed. The increased qualifications provided by this 1988 amendment shall not apply to district judges serving at the time this amendment passes or elected at the general election in 1988.

Section 15. District Court; Judges Pro Tempore

A. Any district judge may hold district court in any county at the request of the judge of such district.

B. Whenever the public business may require, the chief justice of the supreme court shall designate any district judge of the state, or any justice of the supreme court when no district judge may be available within a reasonable time, to hold court in any district, and two or more judges may sit in any district or county separately at the same time.

C. If any district judge is disqualified from hearing any cause or is unable to expeditiously dispose of any cause in the district, the chief justice of the supreme court may designate any retired New

Mexico district judge, court of appeals judge or supreme court justice, with said designees' consent, to hear and determine the cause and to act as district judge pro tempore for such cause.

D. If any judge shall be disqualified from hearing any cause in the district, the parties to such cause, or their attorneys of record, may select some member of the bar to hear and determine said cause, and act as judge pro tempore therein.

Section 16. District Court; Additional Judges; Redistricting

The legislature may increase the number of district judges in any judicial district, and they shall be elected or appointed as other district judges for that district. At any session after the publication of the census of the United States in the year nineteen hundred and twenty, the legislature may rearrange the districts of the state, increase the number thereof, and make provision for a district judge for any additional district.

Section 17. District Court; Judges' Compensation

The legislature shall provide by law for the compensation of the judges of the district court.

Section 18. Disqualification of Judges or Magistrates

No justice, judge or magistrate of any court shall, except by consent of all parties, sit in any cause in which either of the parties are related to him by affinity or consanguinity within the degree of first cousin, or in which he was counsel, or in the trial of which he presided in any inferior court, or in which he has an interest.

Section 19. Ineligibility of Justices or Judges for Nonjudicial Offices

No justice of the supreme court, judge of the court of appeals, judge of the district court or judge of a metropolitan court, while serving, shall be nominated, appointed or elected to any other office in this state except a judicial office.

Section 20. Style of Writs and Processes

All writs and processes shall issue, and all prosecution shall be conducted in the name of "The State of New Mexico."

Section 21. Judges as Conservators of the Peace; Preliminary Examinations in Criminal Cases

Justices of the supreme court, in the state, and district judges and magistrates, in their respective jurisdictions, shall be conservators of the peace. District judges and other judges or magistrates designated by law may hold preliminary examinations in criminal cases.

Section 22. County Clerk as District and Probate Court Clerk
Until otherwise provided by law, a county clerk shall be elected in each county who shall, in the county for which he is elected perform all the duties now performed by the clerks of the district courts and clerks of the probate courts.

Section 23. Probate Court

A probate court is hereby established for each county, which shall be a court of record, and, until otherwise provided by law, shall have the same jurisdiction as heretofore exercised by the probate courts of New Mexico and shall also have jurisdiction to determine heirship with respect to real property in all proceedings for the administration of decedents' estates. The legislature shall have power from time to time to confer upon the probate court in any county in this state jurisdiction to determine heirship in all probate proceedings, and shall have power also from time to time to confer upon the probate court in any county in this state general civil jurisdiction coextensive with the county; provided, however, that such court shall not have jurisdiction in civil causes in which the matter in controversy shall exceed in value three thousand dollars ($3,000.00) exclusive of interest and cost; nor in any action for malicious prosecution, slander and libel; nor in any action against officers for misconduct in office; nor in any action for the specific performance of contracts for the sale of real estate; nor in any action for the possession of land; nor in any matter wherein the title or boundaries of land may be in dispute or drawn in question, except as title to real property may be affected by the determination of heirship; nor to grant writs of injunction, habeas corpus or extraordinary writs. Jurisdiction may be conferred upon the judges of said court to act as examining and committing magistrates in criminal cases, and upon said courts for the trial of misdemeanors in which the punishment cannot be imprisonment in the penitentiary, or in which the fine cannot be in excess of one thousand dollars ($1,000). A jury for the trial of such cases shall consist of six men. The legislature shall prescribe the qualifications and fix the compensation of probate judges.

Section 24. District Attorneys

There shall be a district attorney for each judicial district, who shall be learned in the law, and who shall have been a resident of New Mexico for three years next prior to his election, shall be the law officer of the state and of the counties within his district, shall be elected for a term of four years, and shall perform such duties and receive such salary as may be prescribed by law. The legislature shall have the power to provide for the election of additional district attorneys in any judicial district and to designate the counties therein for which the district attorneys shall serve; but no district attorney shall be elected for any district of which he is not a resident.

Section 25.

Repealed.

Section 26. Magistrate Court

The legislature shall establish a magistrate court to exercise limited original jurisdiction as may be provided by law. The magistrate court shall be composed of such districts and elective magistrates as may be provided by law. Magistrates shall be qualified electors of, and reside in, their respective districts, and the legislature shall prescribe other qualifications. Magistrates shall receive compensation as may be provided by law, which compensation shall not be diminished during their term of office. Metropolitan court judges shall be chosen as provided in this constitution.

Section 27. Appeals from Probate Courts and Other Inferior Courts

Appeals shall be allowed in all cases from the final judgments and decisions of the probate courts and other inferior courts to the district courts, and in all such appeals, trial shall be had de novo unless otherwise provided by law.

Section 28. Court of Appeals; Number, Qualifications, Compensation; Quorum; Majority Concurring in Judgment; Power of Chief Justice to Select Acting Justices

The court of appeals shall consist of not less than seven judges who shall be chosen as provided in this constitution, whose qualifications shall be the same as those of justices of the supreme court and whose compensation shall be as provided by law. The increased qualifications provided by this 1988 amendment shall not apply to court of appeals judges serving at the time this amendment passes or elected at the general election in 1988.

Three judges of the court of appeals shall constitute a quorum for the transaction of business, and a majority of those participating must concur in any judgment of the court. When necessary, the chief justice of the supreme court may designate any justice of the supreme court, or any district judge of the state, to act as a judge of the court of appeals, and the chief justice may designate any judge of the court of appeals to hold court in any district, or to act as a justice of the supreme court.

Section 29. Court of Appeals; Jurisdiction; Issuance of Writs
The court of appeals shall have no original jurisdiction. It may be authorized by law to review directly decisions of administrative agencies of the state, and it may be authorized by rules of the supreme court to issue all writs necessary or appropriate in aid of its appellate jurisdiction. In all other cases, it shall exercise appellate jurisdiction as may be provided by law.

Section 30. Fees Collected by Judiciary Paid to State Treasury
All fees collected by the judicial department shall be paid into the state treasury as may be provided by law and no justice, judge or magistrate of any court shall retain any fees as compensation or otherwise.

Section 31. Justices of the Peace Abolished.

Justices of the peace shall be abolished not later than five years from the effective date of this amendment and may, within this period, be abolished by law, and magistrate courts vested with appropriate jurisdiction. Until so abolished, justices of the peace shall be continued under existing laws.

Section 32. Judicial Standards Commission

There is created the "judicial standards commission", consisting of two justices or judges, one magistrate, one municipal judge and two lawyers selected as may be provided by law to serve for terms of four years, and seven citizens, none of whom is a justice, judge or magistrate of any court or licensed to practice law in this state, who shall be appointed by the governor for five-year staggered terms as may be provided by law. If a position on the commission becomes vacant for any reason, the successor shall be selected by the original appointing authority in the same manner as the original appointment was made and shall serve for the remainder of the term vacated. No act of the commission is valid unless concurred in by a majority of its members. The commission shall select one of the members appointed by the governor to serve as chair. In accordance with this section, any justice, judge or magistrate of any court may be disciplined or removed for willful misconduct in office, persistent failure or inability to perform a judge's duties, or habitual intemperance, or may be retired for disability seriously interfering with the performance of the justice's, judge's or magistrate's duties that is, or is likely to become, of a permanent character. The commission may, after investigation it deems necessary, order a hearing to be held before it concerning the discipline, removal or retirement of a justice, judge or magistrate, or the commission may appoint three masters who are justices or judges of courts of record to hear and take evidence in the matter and to report their findings to the commission. After hearing or after considering the record and the findings and report of the masters, if the commission finds good cause, it shall recommend to the supreme court the discipline, removal or retirement of the justice, judge or magistrate. The supreme court shall review the record of the proceedings on the law and facts and may permit the introduction of additional evidence, and it shall order the discipline, removal or retirement as it finds just and proper or wholly reject the recommendation. Upon an order for retirement, any justice, judge or magistrate participating in a statutory retirement program shall be retired with the same rights as if the justice, judge or magistrate had retired pursuant to the retirement program. Upon an order for removal, the justice, judge or magistrate shall thereby be removed from office, and the justice's, judge's or magistrate's salary shall cease from the date of the order. All papers filed with the commission or its masters, and proceedings before the commission or its masters, are confidential. The filing of papers and giving of testimony before the commission or its masters is privileged in any action for defamation, except that the record filed by the commission in the supreme court continues privileged but, upon its filing, loses its confidential character, and a writing that was privileged prior to its filing with the commission or its masters does not lose its privilege by the filing. The commission shall promulgate regulations establishing procedures for hearings under this section. No justice, judge or magistrate who is a member of the commission or supreme court shall participate in any proceeding involving the justice's, judge's or magistrate's own discipline, removal or retirement. This section is alternative to, and cumulative with, the removal of justices, judges and magistrates by impeachment and the original superintending control of the supreme court.

Section 33. Retention or Rejection at General Election

A. Each justice of the supreme court, judge of the court of appeals, district judge or metropolitan court judge shall have been elected to that position in a partisan election prior to being eligible for a nonpartisan retention election. Thereafter, each such justice or judge shall be subject to retention or rejection on a nonpartisan ballot. Retention of the judicial office shall require at least fifty-seven percent of the vote cast on the question of retention or rejection.

B. Each justice of the supreme court or judge of the court of appeals shall be subject to retention or rejection in like manner at the general election every eighth year.

C. Each district judge shall be subject to retention or rejection in like manner at the general election every sixth year.

D. Each metropolitan court judge shall be subject to retention or rejection in like manner at the general election every fourth year.

E. Every justice of the supreme court, judge of the court of appeals, district judge or metropolitan court judge holding office on January 1 next following the date of the election at which this amendment is adopted shall be deemed to have fulfilled the requirements of Subsection A of this section and the justice or judge shall be eligible for retention or rejection by the electorate at the general election next preceding the end of the term of which the justice or judge was last elected prior to the adoption of this amendment.

Section 34. Vacancies in Office; Date for Filing Declaration of Candidacy

The office of any justice or judge subject to the provisions of Article 6, Section 33 of this constitution becomes vacant on January 1 immediately following the general election at which the justice or judge is rejected by more than forty-three percent of those voting on the question of retention or rejection or on January 1 immediately following the date the justice or judge fails to file a declaration of candidacy for the retention of the justice's or judge's office in the general election at which the justice or judge would be subject to retention or rejection by the electorate. Otherwise, the office becomes vacant upon the date of the death, resignation or removal by impeachment of the justice or judge.

Section 35. Appellate Judges Nominating Commission

There is created the "appellate judges nominating commission," consisting of: the chief justice of the supreme court or the chief justice's designee from the supreme court; two judges of the court of appeals appointed by the chief judge of the court of appeals; the governor, the speaker of the house of representatives and the president pro tempore of the senate shall each appoint two persons, one of whom shall be an attorney licensed to practice law in this state and the other who shall be a citizen who is not licensed to practice law in any state; the dean of the university of New Mexico school of law, who shall serve as chairman of the commission and shall vote only in the event of a tie vote; four members of the state bar of New Mexico, representing civil and criminal prosecution and defense, appointed by the president of the state bar and the judges on this committee. The appointments shall be made in such manner that each of the two largest major political parties, as defined by the Election Code, shall be equally represented on the commission. If necessary, the president of the state bar and the judges on this committee shall make the minimum number of additional appointments of members of the state bar as is necessary to make each of the two largest major political parties be equally represented on the commission. These additional members of the state bar shall be appointed such that the diverse interests of the state bar are represented. The dean of the university of New Mexico school of law shall be the final arbiter of whether such diverse interests are represented. Members of the commission shall be appointed for terms as may be provided by law. If a position on the commission becomes vacant for any reason, the successor shall be selected by the original appointing authority in the same manner as the original appointment was made and shall serve for the remainder of the term vacated.

The commission shall actively solicit, accept and evaluate applications from qualified lawyers for the position of justice of the supreme court or judge of the court of appeals and may require an applicant to submit any information it deems relevant to the consideration of his application.

Upon the occurrence of an actual vacancy in the office of justice of the supreme court or judge of the court of appeals, the commission shall meet within thirty days and within that period submit to the governor the names of persons qualified for the judicial office and recommended for appointment to that office by a majority of the commission.

Immediately after receiving the commission nominations, the governor may make one request of the commission for submission of additional names, and the commission shall promptly submit such additional names if a majority of the commission finds that additional persons would be qualified and recommends those persons for appointment to the judicial office. The governor shall fill a vacancy or appoint a successor to fill an impending vacancy in the office of justice of the supreme court or judge of the court of appeals within thirty days after receiving final nominations from the commission by appointing one of the persons nominated by the commission for appointment to that office. If the governor fails to make the appointment within that period or from those nominations, the appointment shall be made from those nominations by the chief justice or the acting chief justice of the supreme court. Any person appointed shall serve until the next general election. That person's successor shall be chosen at such election and shall hold the office until the expiration of the original term.

Section 36. District Court Judges Nominating Committee

There is created the "district court judges nominating committee" for each judicial district. Each and every provision of Section 35 of Article 6 of this constitution shall apply to the "district judges nominating committee" except that: the chief judge of the district court of that judicial district or the chief judge's designee from that district court shall sit on the committee; there shall be only one appointment from the court of appeals; and the citizen members and state bar members shall be persons who reside in that judicial district.

Section 37. Metropolitan Court Judges Nominating Committee

There is created the "metropolitan court judges nominating committee" for each metropolitan court. Each and every provision of Section 35 of Article 6 of this constitution shall apply to the metropolitan court judicial nominating committee except that: no judge of the court of appeals shall sit on the committee; the chief judge of the district court of the judicial district in which the metropolitan court is located or the chief judge's designee from that district court shall sit on the committee; the chief judge of that metropolitan court or the chief judge's designee from that metropolitan court shall sit on the committee only in the case of a vacancy in a metropolitan court; and the citizen members and state bar members shall be persons who reside in the judicial district in which that metropolitan court is located.

Section 38. Chief Judge of District and Metropolitan Court Districts

Each judicial district and metropolitan court district shall have a chief judge who shall have the administrative responsibility for that judicial district or metropolitan court district. Each chief judge shall be selected by a majority of the district judges or, in the case of the metropolitan court, by a majority of the metropolitan court judges in that judicial district or metropolitan court district. In the event of a tie, the senior judge shall be the chief judge.

Section 39. Creation of public defender department and public defender commission

A. A "public defender department" is established as an independent state agency. The chief public defender is the administrative head of the public defender department. The term and qualifications of the chief public defender shall be as provided by law.

B. The "public defender commission" is established. The public defender commission shall appoint the chief public defender. The public defender commission shall exercise independent oversight of the department and provide guidance to the chief public defender in the administration of the department and the representation of indigent persons. The commission shall not interfere with the discretion or the professional judgment or advocacy of a public defender office, a public defender contractor or assigned counsel in the representation of individual cases. Terms, qualifications and membership of the public defender commission shall be as provided by law.

ARTICLE VII: ELECTIVE FRANCHISE

Section 1. Qualifications of Voters; Absentee Voting; School Elections; Registration

Every person who is a qualified elector pursuant to the constitution and laws of the United States and a citizen thereof shall be qualified to vote in all elections in New Mexico, subject to residency and registration requirements provided by law, except as restricted by statute either by reason of criminal conviction for a felony or by reason of mental incapacity, being limited only to those persons who are unable to mark their ballot and who are concurrently also unable to communicate their voting preference.

The legislature may enact laws providing for absentee voting by qualified electors. All school elections shall be held at different times from other elections. The legislature shall have the power to require the registration of the qualified electors as a requisite for voting and shall regulate the manner, time and places of voting. The legislature shall enact such laws as will secure the secrecy of the ballot and the purity of elections and guard against the abuse of elective franchise. Not more than two members of the board of registration and not more than two judges of election shall belong to the same political party at the time of their appointment.

Section 2. Qualifications for Holding Office

A. Every citizen of the United States who is a legal resident of the state and is a qualified elector therein, shall be qualified to hold any elective public office except as otherwise provided in this constitution.

B. The legislature may provide by law for such qualifications and standards as may be necessary for holding an appointive position by any public officer or employee.

C. The right to hold public office in New Mexico shall not be denied or abridged on account of sex, and wherever the masculine gender is used in this constitution, in defining the qualifications for specific offices, it shall be construed to include the feminine gender. The payment of public road poll tax, school poll tax or service on juries shall not be made a prerequisite to the right of a person to vote or hold office.

Section 3. Religious and Racial Equality Protected; Restrictions on Amendments

The right of any citizen of the state to vote, hold office or sit upon juries, shall never be restricted, abridged or impaired on account of religion, race, language or color, or inability to speak, read or write the English or Spanish languages except as may be otherwise provided in this constitution; and the provisions of this section and of Section One of this article shall never be amended except upon a vote of the people of this state in an election at which at least three-fourths of the electors voting in the whole state, and at least two-thirds of those voting in each county of the state, shall vote for such amendment.

Section 4. Residence
No person shall be deemed to have acquired or lost residence by reason of his presence or absence while employed in the service of the United States or of the state, nor while a student at any school.

Section 5. Election by Ballot; Plurality Elects Candidate

A. All elections shall be by ballot.

B. The legislature may provide by law for runoff elections for all elections other than municipal, primary or statewide elections. If the legislature does not provide for runoff elections, the person who receives the highest number of votes for any office, except as provided in this section, and except in the cases of the offices of governor and lieutenant governor, shall be declared elected to that office. The joint candidates receiving the highest number of votes for the offices of governor and lieutenant governor shall be declared elected to those offices.

C. In a municipal election, the candidate that receives the most votes for an office shall be declared elected to that office, unless the municipality has provided for runoff elections. A municipality may provide for runoff elections as follows:

(1) a municipality that has not adopted a charter pursuant to Article 10, Section 6 of the constitution of New Mexico may provide by ordinance for runoff elections;

(2) a municipality that has adopted a charter pursuant to Article 10, Section 6 of the constitution of New Mexico, and prior to the adoption of this amendment the charter provided for runoff elections, shall hold runoff elections pursuant to the charter; or

(3) a municipality that adopts or has adopted a charter pursuant to Article 10, Section 6 of the constitution of New Mexico may, subsequent to the adoption of this amendment, provide for runoff elections as provided in its charter.

ARTICLE VIII: TAXATION AND REVENUE

Section 1. Levy to Be Proportionate to Value; Uniform and Equal Taxes; Percentage of Value Taxed; Limitation on Annual Valuation Increases

A. Except as provided in Subsection B of this section, taxes levied upon tangible property shall be in proportion to the value thereof, and taxes shall be equal and uniform upon subjects of taxation of the same class. Different methods may be provided by law to determine value of different kinds of property, but the percentage of value against which tax rates are assessed shall not exceed thirty-three and one-third percent.
B. The legislature shall provide by law for the valuation of residential property for property taxation purposes in a manner that limits annual increases in valuation of residential property. The limitation may be applied to classes of residential property taxpayers based on owner-occupancy, age or income. The limitations may be authorized statewide or at the option of a local jurisdiction and may include conditions under which the limitation is applied. Any valuation limitations authorized as a local jurisdiction option shall provide for applying statewide or multi-jurisdictional property tax rates to the value of the property as if the valuation increase limitation did not apply.

Section 2. Property Tax Limits; Exception

Taxes levied upon real or personal property for state revenue shall not exceed four mills annually on each dollar of the assessed valuation thereof except for the support of the educational, penal and charitable institutions of the state, payment of the state debt and interest thereon; and the total annual tax levy upon such property for all state purposes exclusive of necessary levies for the state debt shall not exceed ten mills; provided, however, that taxes levied upon real or personal tangible property for all purposes, except special levies on specific classes of property and except necessary levies for public debt, shall not exceed twenty mills annually on each dollar of the assessed valuation thereof, but laws may be passed authorizing additional taxes to be levied outside of such limitation when approved by at least a majority of the qualified electors of the taxing district who paid a property tax therein during the preceding year voting on such proposition.

Section 3. Tax-Exempt Property

The property of the United States, the state and all counties, towns, cities and school districts and other municipal corporations, public libraries, community ditches and all laterals thereof, all church property not used for commercial purposes, all property used for educational or charitable purposes, all cemeteries not used or held for private or corporate profit and all bonds of the state of New Mexico, and of the counties, municipalities and districts thereof shall be exempt from taxation. Provided, however, that any property acquired by public libraries, community ditches and all laterals thereof, property acquired by churches, property acquired and used for educational or charitable purposes, and property acquired by cemeteries not used or held for private, or corporate profit, and property acquired by the Indian service and property acquired by the United States government or by the state of New Mexico by outright purchase or trade, where such property was, prior to such transfer, subject to the lien of any tax or assessment for the principal or interest of any bonded indebtedness shall not be exempt from such lien, nor from the payment of such taxes or assessments.

Exemptions of personal property from ad valorem taxation may be provided by law if approved by a three-fourths majority vote of all the members elected to each house of the legislature.

Section 4. Misuse and Deposit of Public Money

Any public officer making any profit out of public money or using the same for any purpose not authorized by law, shall be deemed guilty of a felony and shall be punished as provided by law and shall be disqualified to hold public office. All public money not invested in interest-bearing securities shall be deposited in national banks in this state, in banks or trust companies incorporated under the laws of the state, in federal savings and loan associations in this state, in savings and loan associations incorporated under the laws of this state whose deposits are insured by an agency of the United States and in credit unions incorporated under the laws of this state or the United States to the extent that such deposits of public money in credit unions are insured by an agency of the United States, and the interest derived therefrom shall be applied in the manner prescribed by law. The conditions of such deposits shall be provided by law.

Section 5. Head of Family and Veteran Exemptions

The legislature shall exempt from taxation the property of each head of the family in the amount of two thousand dollars ($2,000). The legislature shall also exempt from taxation the property, including the community or joint property of husband and wife, of every honorably discharged member of the armed forces of the United States and the widow or widower of every such honorably discharged member of the armed forces of the United States, in the sum of three thousand dollars ($3,000) in 2004; three thousand five hundred dollars ($3,500) in 2005; and four thousand dollars ($4,000) in 2006 and each subsequent year. Provided, that in every case where exemption is claimed on the ground of the claimant's having served with the armed forces of the United States as aforesaid, the burden of proving actual and bona fide ownership of such property upon which exemption is claimed, shall be upon the claimant.

Section 6. Assessment of Lands

Lands held in large tracts shall not be assessed for taxation at any lower value per acre then [than] lands of the same character or quality and similarly situated, held in smaller tracts. The plowing of land shall not be considered as adding value thereto for the purpose of taxation.

Section 7. Judgments Against Local Officials

No execution shall issue upon judgment rendered against the board of county commissioners of any county, or against any incorporated city, town or village, school district or board of education; or against any officer of any county, incorporated city, town or village, school district or board of education, upon any judgment recovered against him in his official capacity and for which the county, incorporated city, town or village, school district or board of education, is liable, but the same shall be paid out of the proceeds of a tax levy as other liabilities of counties, incorporated cities, towns or villages, school districts or boards of education, and when so collected shall be paid by the county treasurer to the judgment creditor.

Section 8. Exemption of Certain Personalty in Transit Through the State

Personal property which is moving in interstate commerce through or over the state of New Mexico, or which was consigned to a warehouse, public or private, or factory within New Mexico from outside the state for storage in transit to a final destination outside the state of New Mexico, manufacturing, processing or fabricating while in transit to a final destination, whether specified when transportation begins or afterwards, which destination is also outside the state, shall be deemed not to have acquired a situs in New Mexico for purposes of taxation and shall be exempt from taxation. Such property shall not be deprived of such exemption because while in the warehouse the property is assembled, bound, joined, processed, disassembled, divided, cut, broken in bulk, relabeled or repackaged.

Section 9. Elected Governing Authority Prerequisite to Levy of Tax

No tax or assessment of any kind shall be levied by any political subdivision whose enabling legislation does not provide for an elected governing authority. This section does not prohibit the levying or collection of a tax or special assessment by an initial appointed governing authority where the appointed governing authority will be replaced by an elected one within six years of the date the appointed authority takes office. The provisions of this section shall not be effective until July 1, 1976.

Section 10. Severance Tax Permanent Fund

A. There shall be deposited in a permanent trust fund known as the "severance tax permanent fund" that part of state revenue derived from excise taxes that have been or shall be designated severance taxes imposed upon the severance of natural resources within this state, in excess of that amount that has been or shall be reserved by statute for the payment of principal and interest on outstanding bonds to which severance tax revenue has been or shall be pledged. Money in the severance tax permanent fund shall be invested as provided by law. Distributions from the fund shall be appropriated by the legislature as other general operating revenue is appropriated for the benefit of the people of the state.

B. All additions to the fund and all earnings, including interest, dividends and capital gains from investment of the fund shall be credited to the corpus of the fund.

C. The annual distributions from the fund shall be one hundred two percent of the amount distributed in the immediately preceding fiscal year until the annual distributions equal four and seven-tenths percent of the average of the year-end market values of the fund for the immediately preceding five calendar years. Thereafter, the amount of the annual distributions shall be four and seven-tenths percent of the average of the year-end market values of the fund for the immediately preceding five calendar years.

D. The frequency and the time of the distributions made pursuant to Subsection C of this section shall be as provided by law.

Sections 11 – 14.

Repealed.

Section 15. Property Tax Exemption for Disabled Veterans

The legislature shall exempt from taxation the property, including the community or joint property of husband and wife, of every veteran of the armed forces of the United States who has been determined pursuant to federal law to have a one hundred percent permanent and total service-connected disability, if the veteran occupies the property as his principal place of residence. The legislature shall also provide this exemption from taxation for property owned by the widow or widower of a veteran who was eligible for the exemption provided in this section, if the widow or widower continues to occupy the property as his principal place of residence. The burden of proving eligibility for the exemption in this section is on the person claiming the exemption.

Section 16. Property tax exemption for property of veterans' organization chartered by United States Congress

The legislature shall exempt from taxation the property of a veterans' organization chartered by the United States congress and used primarily for veterans and their families. The burden of proving eligibility for the exemption in this section is on the person claiming the exemption.

ARTICLE IX: STATE, COUNTY AND MUNICIPAL INDEBTEDNESS

Section 1. Debts of Territory and Its Counties Assumed

The state hereby assumes the debts and liabilities of the territory of New Mexico, and the debts of the counties thereof, which were valid and subsisting on June twentieth, nineteen hundred and ten, and pledges its faith and credit for the payment thereof. The legislature shall, at its first session, provide for the payment or refunding thereof by the issue and sale of bonds, or otherwise.

Section 2. Payment of County Debts by Another County

No county shall be required to pay any portion of the debt of any other county so assumed by the state, and the bonds of Grant and Santa Fe counties which were validated, approved and confirmed by act of congress of January sixteenth, eighteen hundred and ninety-seven, shall be paid as hereinafter provided.

Section 3. State Refunding Bonds for Assumed Debts

The bonds authorized by law to provide for the payment of such indebtedness shall be issued in three series, as follows:

Series A. To provide for the payment of such debts and liabilities of the territory of New Mexico.

Series B. To provide for the payment of such debts of said counties.

Series C. To provide for the payment of the bonds and accrued interest thereon of Grant and Santa Fe counties which were validated, approved and confirmed by act of congress, January sixteenth, eighteen hundred and ninety-seven.

Section 4. Sale of Lands for Certain Bond Payments

The proper officers of the state shall, as soon as practicable, select and locate the one million acres of land granted to the state by congress for the payment of the said bonds of Grant and Santa Fe counties, and sell the same or sufficient thereof to pay the interest and principal of the bonds of Series C issued as provided in Section Three hereof. The proceeds of rentals and sales of said land shall be kept in a separate fund and applied to the payment of the interest and principal of the bonds of Series C. Whenever there is not sufficient money in said fund to meet the interest and sinking fund requirements therefore, the deficiency shall be paid out of any funds of the state not otherwise appropriated, and shall be repaid to the state or to the several counties which may have furnished any portion thereof under a general levy, out of the proceeds subsequently received of rentals and sales of said lands.

Any money received by the state from rentals and sales of said lands in excess of the amounts required for the purposes above-mentioned shall be paid into the current and permanent school funds of the state respectively.

Section 5. Remission of County Debts to State Prohibited

The legislature shall never enact any law releasing any county, or any of the taxable property therein, from its obligation to pay to the state any moneys expended by the state by reason of its assumption or payment of the debt of such county.

Section 6. Militia Warrants

No law shall ever be passed by the legislature validating or legalizing, directly or indirectly, the militia warrants alleged to be outstanding against the territory of New Mexico, or any portion thereof; and no such warrant shall be prima facie or conclusive evidence of the validity of the debt purporting to be evidenced thereby or by any other militia warrant. This provision shall not be construed as authorizing any suit against the state.

Section 7. State Indebtedness; Purposes

The state may borrow money not exceeding the sum of two hundred thousand dollars [($200,000)] in the aggregate to meet casual deficits or failure in revenue, or for necessary expenses. The state may also contract debts to suppress insurrection and to provide for the public defense.

Section 8. State Indebtedness; Restrictions

A. No debt other than those specified in the preceding section shall be contracted by or on behalf of this state, unless authorized by law for some specified work or object; which law shall provide for an annual tax levy sufficient to pay the interest and to provide a sinking fund to pay the principal of such debt within fifty years from the time of the contracting thereof. No such law shall take effect until it shall have been submitted to the qualified electors of the state and have received a majority of all the votes cast thereon at a general election; such law shall be published in full in at least one newspaper in each county of the state, if one be published therein, once each week, for four successive weeks next preceding such election. No debt shall be so created if the total indebtedness of the state, exclusive of the debts of the territory, and the several counties thereof, assumed by the state, would thereby be made to exceed one percent of the assessed valuation of all the property subject to taxation in the state as shown by the preceding general assessment.
B. For the purposes of this section and Article 4, Section 29 of the constitution of New Mexico, a financing agreement entered into by the state for the leasing of a building or other real property with an option to purchase for a price that is reduced according to the payments made by the state pursuant to the financing agreement is not a debt if:

(1) there is no legal obligation for the state to continue the lease from year to year or to purchase the real property; and

(2) the agreement provides that the lease shall be terminated if sufficient appropriations are not available to meet the current lease payments.

Section 9. Use of Borrowed Funds

Any money borrowed by the state, or any county, district or municipality thereof, shall be applied to the purpose for which it was obtained, or to repay such loan, and to no other purpose whatever.

Section 10. County Indebtedness; Restrictions

No county shall borrow money except for the following purposes:

A. erecting, remodeling and making additions to necessary public buildings;

B. constructing or repairing public roads and bridges and purchasing capital equipment for such projects;

C. constructing or acquiring a system for supplying water, including the acquisition of water and water rights, necessary real estate or rights-of-way and easements;

D. constructing or acquiring a sewer system, including the necessary real estate or rights-of-way and easements;

E. constructing an airport or sanitary landfill, including the necessary real estate;

F. acquiring necessary real estate for open space, open space trails and related areas and facilities; or

G. the purchase of books and other library resources for libraries in the county.

In such cases, indebtedness shall be incurred only after the proposition to create such debt has been submitted to the registered voters of the county and approved by a majority of those voting thereon. No bonds issued for such purpose shall run for more than fifty years. Provided, however, that no money derived from general obligation bonds issued and sold hereunder shall be used for maintaining existing buildings and, if so, such bonds shall be invalid.

Section 11. School District Indebtedness; Restrictions

A. Except as provided in Subsection C of this section, no school district shall borrow money except for the purpose of erecting, remodeling, making additions to and furnishing school buildings or purchasing or improving school grounds or any combination of these purposes, and in such cases only when the proposition to create the debt has been submitted to a vote of such qualified electors of the district as are owners of real estate within the school district and a majority of those voting on the question has voted in favor of creating such debt.

B. No school district shall ever become indebted in an amount exceeding six percent on the assessed valuation of the taxable property within the school district as shown by the preceding general assessment.

C. A school district may create a debt by entering into a lease-purchase arrangement to acquire education technology equipment without submitting the proposition to a vote of the qualified electors of the district, but any debt created is subject to the limitation of Subsection B of this section.

D. For the purposes of this section, a financing agreement entered into by a school district or a charter school for the leasing of a building or other real property with an option to purchase for a price that is reduced according to the payments made by the school district or charter school pursuant to the financing agreement is not a debt if:

(1) there is no legal obligation for the school district or charter school to continue the lease from year to year or to purchase the real property; and

(2) the agreement provides that the lease shall be terminated if sufficient money is not available to meet the current lease payments.

Section 12. Municipal Indebtedness; Restrictions

No city, town or village shall contract any debt except by an ordinance, which shall be irrepealable until the indebtedness therein provided for shall have been fully paid or discharged, and which shall specify the purposes to which the funds to be raised shall be applied, and which shall provide for the levy of a tax, not exceeding twelve mills on the dollar upon all taxable property within such city, town or village, sufficient to pay the interest on, and to extinguish the principal of, such debt within fifty years. The proceeds of such tax shall be applied only to the payment of such interest and principal. No such debt shall be created unless the question of incurring the same shall, at a regular election for councilmen, aldermen or other officers of such city, town or village, or at any special election called for such purpose, have been submitted to a vote of such qualified electors thereof as have paid a property tax therein during the preceding year, and a majority of those voting on the question by ballot deposited in a separate ballot box when voting in a regular election, shall have voted in favor of creating such debt. A proposal which does not receive the required number of votes for adoption at any special election called for that purpose, shall not be resubmitted in any special election within a period of one year. For the purpose, only, of voting on the creation of the debt, any person owning property within the corporate limits of the city, town or village who has paid a property tax therein during the preceding year and who is otherwise qualified to vote in the county where such city, town or village is situated shall be a qualified elector.

Section 13. County and Municipal Debt Limit; Exceptions

No county, city, town or village shall ever become indebted to an amount in the aggregate, including existing indebtedness, exceeding four per centum on the value of the taxable property within such county, city, town or village, as shown by the last preceding assessment for state or county taxes; and all bonds or obligations issued in excess of such amount shall be void; provided, that any city, town or village may contract debts in excess of such limitation for the construction or purchase of a system for supplying water, or of a sewer system, for such city, town or village.

Section 14. Aid to Private Enterprise; Veterans Scholarship Programs; Student Loans; Job Opportunities; Affordable Housing

Neither the state nor any county, school district or municipality, except as otherwise provided in this constitution, shall directly or indirectly lend or pledge its credit or make any donation to or in aid of any person, association or public or private corporation or in aid of any private enterprise for the construction of any railroad except as provided in Subsections A through G of this section.

A. Nothing in this section prohibits the state or any county or municipality from making provision for the care and maintenance of sick and indigent persons.

B. Nothing in this section prohibits the state from establishing a veterans' scholarship program for Vietnam conflict veterans who are post-secondary students at educational institutions under the exclusive control of the state by exempting such veterans from the payment of tuition. For the purposes of this subsection, a "Vietnam conflict veteran" is any person who has been honorably discharged from the armed forces of the United States, who was a resident of New Mexico at the original time of entry into the armed forces from New Mexico or who has lived in New Mexico for ten years or more and who has been awarded a Vietnam campaign medal for service in the armed forces of this country in Vietnam during the period from August 5, 1964 to the official termination date of the Vietnam conflict as designated by executive order of the president of the United States.

C. The state may establish by law a program of loans to students of the healing arts, as defined by law, for residents of the state who, in return for the payment of educational expenses, contract with the state to practice their profession for a period of years after graduation within areas of the state designated by law.

D. Nothing in this section prohibits the state or a county or municipality from creating new job opportunities by providing land, buildings or infrastructure for facilities to support new or expanding businesses if this assistance is granted pursuant to general implementing legislation that is approved by a majority vote of those elected to each house of the legislature. The implementing legislation shall include adequate safeguards to protect public money or other resources used for the purposes authorized in this subsection. The implementing legislation shall further provide that:

(1) each specific county or municipal project providing assistance pursuant to this subsection need not be approved by the legislature but shall be approved by the county or municipality pursuant to procedures provided in the implementing legislation; and

(2) each specific state project providing assistance pursuant to this subsection shall be approved by law.

E. Nothing in this section prohibits the state, or the instrumentality of the state designated by the legislature as the state's housing authority, or a county or a municipality from:

(1) donating or otherwise providing or paying a portion of the costs of land for the construction on it of affordable housing;

(2) donating or otherwise providing or paying a portion of the costs of construction or renovation of affordable housing or the costs of conversion or renovation of buildings into affordable housing; or

(3) providing or paying the costs of financing or infrastructure necessary to support affordable housing projects.

F. The provisions of Subsection E of this section are not self-executing. Before the described assistance may be provided, enabling legislation shall be enacted by a majority vote of the members elected to each house of the legislature. This enabling legislation shall:

(1) define "affordable housing";

(2) establish eligibility criteria for the recipients of land, buildings and infrastructure;

(3) contain provisions to ensure the successful completion of affordable housing projects supported by assistance authorized pursuant to Subsection E of this section;

(4) require a county or municipality providing assistance pursuant to Subsection E of this section to give prior formal approval by ordinance for a specific affordable housing assistance grant and include in the ordinance the conditions of the grant;

(5) require prior approval by law of an affordable housing assistance grant by the state; and

(6) require the governing body of the instrumentality of the state, designated by the legislature as the state's housing authority, to give prior approval, by resolution, for affordable housing grants that are to be given by the instrumentality.

G. Nothing in this section prohibits the state from establishing a veterans' scholarship program, for military war veterans who are post-secondary students at educational institutions under the exclusive control of the state and who have exhausted all educational benefits offered by the United States department of defense or the United States department of veterans affairs, by exempting such veterans from the payment of tuition. For the purposes of this subsection, a "military war veteran" is any person who has been honorably discharged from the armed forces of the United States, who was a resident of New Mexico at the original time of entry into the armed forces or who has lived in New Mexico for ten years or more and who has been awarded a southwest Asia service medal, global war on terror service medal, Iraq campaign medal, Afghanistan campaign medal or any other medal issued for service in the armed forces of this country in support of any United States military campaign or armed conflict as defined by congress or by presidential executive order or any other campaign medal issued for service after August 1, 1990 in the armed forces of the United States during periods of armed conflict as defined by congress or by executive order.

Section 15. State and Local Refunding Bonds

Nothing in this article shall be construed to prohibit the issue of bonds for the purpose of paying or refunding any valid state, county, district or municipal bonds and it shall not be necessary to submit the question of the issue of such bonds to a vote as herein provided.

Section 16. State Highway Bonds

Laws enacted by the fifth legislature authorizing the issue and sale of state highway bonds for the purpose of providing funds for the construction and improvement of state highways and to enable the state to meet and secure allotments of federal funds to aid in construction and improvement of roads, and laws so enacted authorizing the issue and sale of state highway debentures to anticipate the collection of revenues from motor vehicle licenses and other revenues provided by law for the state road fund, shall take effect without submitting them to the electors of the state, and notwithstanding that the total indebtedness of the state may thereby temporarily exceed one per centum of the assessed valuation of all the property subject to taxation in the state. Provided, that the total amount of such state highway bonds payable from proceeds of taxes levied on property outstanding at any one time shall not exceed two million dollars [($2,000,000)]. The legislature shall not enact any law which will decrease the amount of the annual revenues pledged for the payment of state highway debentures or which will divert any of such revenues to any other purpose so long as any of the said debentures issued to anticipate the collection thereof remain unpaid.

ARTICLE X: COUNTY AND MUNICIPAL CORPORATIONS

Section 1. Classification of Counties; Salaries and Fees of County Officers

The legislature shall at its first session classify the counties and fix salaries for all county officers, which shall also apply to those elected at the first election under this constitution. And no county officer shall receive to his own use any fees or emoluments other than the annual salary provided by law, and all fees earned by any officer shall be by him collected and paid into the treasury of the county.

Section 1. Classification of Counties; Salaries and Fees of County Officers

The legislature shall at its first session classify the counties and fix salaries for all county officers, which shall also apply to those elected at the first election under this constitution. And no county officer shall receive to his own use any fees or emoluments other than the annual salary provided by law, and all fees earned by any officer shall be by him collected and paid into the treasury of the county.

Section 2. Terms of County Officers

A. In every county all elected officials shall serve four-year terms, subject to the provisions of Subsection B of this section.

B. In those counties that prior to 1992 have not had four-year terms for elected officials, the assessor, sheriff and probate judge shall be elected to four-year terms and the treasurer and clerk shall be elected to two-year terms in the first election following the adoption of this amendment. In subsequent elections, the treasurer and clerk shall be elected to four-year terms.

C. To provide for staggered county commission terms, in counties with three county commissioners, the terms of no more than two commissioners shall expire in the same year; and in counties with five county commissioners, the terms of no more than three commissioners shall expire in the same year.

D. All county officers, after having served two consecutive four-year terms, shall be ineligible to hold any county office for two years thereafter.

Section 3. Removal of County Seats

No county seat, where there are county buildings, shall be removed unless three-fifths of the votes cast by qualified electors on the question of removal at an election called and held as now or hereafter provided by law, be in favor of such removal. The proposition of removal shall not be submitted in the same county oftener than once in eight years.

Section 4. Combined City and County Corporations

A. The legislature shall, by general law, provide for the formation of combined city and county municipal corporations, and for the manner of determining the territorial limits thereof, each of which shall be known as a "city and county," and, when organized, shall contain a population of at least fifty thousand (50,000) inhabitants. No such city and county shall be formed except by a majority vote of the qualified electors of the area proposed to be included therein, and if the proposed area includes any area not within the existing limits of a city, a majority of those electors living outside the city, voting separately shall be required. Any such city and county shall be permitted to frame a charter for its own government, and amend the same, in the manner provided by the legislature by general law for the formation and organization of such corporations.

B. Every such charter shall designate the respective officers of such city and county who shall perform the duties imposed by law upon county officers and shall make provisions for the payment of existing city and county indebtedness as hereinafter required. The officers of a city and county, their compensation, qualifications, term of office and manner of election or appointment, shall be as provided for in its charter, subject to general laws and applicable constitutional provisions. The salary of any elective or appointive officer of a city and county shall not be changed after his election or appointment or during his term of office; nor shall the term of any such officer be extended beyond the period for which he is elected or appointed. Every such city and county shall have and enjoy all rights, powers and privileges asserted in its charter not inconsistent with its general laws, and, in addition thereto, such rights, powers and privileges as may be granted to it, or possessed and enjoyed by cities and counties of like population separately organized.

C. No city or county government existing outside the territorial limits of such city and county shall exercise any police, taxation or other powers within the territorial limits of such city and county, but all such powers shall be exercised by the city and county and the officers thereof, subject to such constitutional provisions and general laws as apply to either cities or counties.

D. In case an existing county is divided in the formation of city and county government, such city and county shall be liable for a just proportion of the existing debts or liabilities of the former county and shall account for and pay the county remaining a just proportion of the value of any real estate or other property owned by the former county and taken over by the city and county government, the method of determining such proportion shall be prescribed by general law, but such division shall not affect the rights of creditors.

E. Nothing herein contained shall be construed to alter or amend the existing constitutional provisions regarding apportionment of representation in the legislature or in the boundaries of legislative districts or judicial districts, nor the jurisdiction or organization of the district or probate courts.

Section 5. Incorporated Counties

Any county at the time of the adoption of this amendment, which is less than one hundred forty-four square miles in area and has a population of ten thousand or more may become an incorporated county by the following procedure:

A. upon the filing of a petition containing the signatures of at least ten percent of the registered voters in the county, the board of county commissioners shall appoint a charter commission consisting of not less than three persons to draft an incorporated county charter; or

B. the board of county commissioners may, upon its own initiative, appoint a charter commission consisting of not less than three persons to draft an incorporated county charter; and

C. the proposed charter drafted by the charter commission shall be submitted to the qualified voters of the county within one year after the appointment of the commission and if adopted by a majority of the qualified voters voting in the election the county shall become an incorporated county.

The charter of an incorporated county shall provide for the form and organization of the incorporated county government and shall designate those officers which shall be elected, and those officers and employees which shall perform the duties assigned by law to county officers.

An incorporated county may exercise all powers and shall be subject to all limitations granted to municipalities by Article 9, Section 12 of the constitution of New Mexico and all powers granted to municipalities by statute.

A charter of an incorporated county shall be amended in accordance with the provisions of the charter.
Nothing herein contained shall be construed to alter or amend the existing constitutional provisions regarding apportionment of representation in the legislature or in the boundaries of legislative districts or judicial districts, nor the jurisdiction or organization of the district or probate courts.

The provisions of this amendment shall be self-executing.

Section 6. Municipal Home Rule

A. For the purpose of electing some or all of the members of the governing body of a municipality:

(1) the legislature may authorize a municipality by general law to be districted;

(2) if districts have not been established as authorized by law, the governing body of a municipality may, by resolution, authorize the districting of the municipality. The resolution shall not become effective in the municipality until approved by a majority vote in the municipality; and

(3) if districts have not been established as authorized by law or by resolution, the voters of a municipality, by a petition which is signed by not less than five percent of the registered qualified electors of the municipality and which specified the number of members of the governing body to be elected from districts, may require the governing body to submit to the registered qualified electors of the municipality, at the next regular municipal election held not less than sixty days after the petition is filed, a resolution requiring the districting of the municipality by its governing body. The resolution shall not become effective in the municipality until approved by a majority vote in the municipality. The signatures for a petition shall be collected within a six-months period.

B. Any member of the governing body of a municipality representing a district shall be a resident of, and elected by, the registered qualified electors of that district.

C. The registered qualified electors of a municipality may adopt, amend or repeal a charter in the manner provided by law. In the absence of law, the governing body of a municipality may appoint a charter commission upon its own initiative or shall appoint a charter commission upon the filing of a petition containing the signatures of at least five percent of the registered qualified electors of the municipality. The charter commission shall consist of not less than seven members who shall draft a proposed charter. The proposed charter shall be submitted to the registered qualified electors of the municipality within one year after the appointment of the charter commission. If the charter is approved by a majority vote in the municipality, it shall become effective at the time and in the manner provided in the charter.

D. A municipality which adopts a charter may exercise all legislative powers and perform all functions not expressly denied by general law or charter. This grant of powers shall not include the power to enact private or civil laws governing civil relationships except as incident to the exercise of an independent municipal power, nor shall it include the power to provide for a penalty greater than the penalty provided for a petty misdemeanor. No tax imposed by the governing body of a charter municipality, except a tax authorized by general law, shall become effective until approved by a majority vote in the charter municipality.

E. The purpose of this section is to provide for maximum local self-government. A liberal construction shall be given to the powers of municipalities.

Section 7. Five-Member Boards of County Commissioners

The board of county commissioners by unanimous vote may adopt an ordinance to increase the size of the boards of county commissioners to five members. Upon creation of a five-member board, the county shall be divided by the incumbent board of county commissioners into five county commission districts that shall be compact, contiguous and as nearly equal in population as practicable. One county commissioner shall reside within and be elected from each county commission district. Change of residence to a place outside the district from which a county commissioner was elected shall automatically terminate the service of that commissioner and the office shall be declared vacant.

Section 8. New Activity or Service Mandated by State Rule or Regulation

A state rule or regulation mandating any county or city to engage in any new activity, to provide any new service or to increase any current level of activity or to provide any service beyond that required by existing law, shall not have the force of law, unless, or until, the state provides sufficient new funding or a means of new funding to the county or city to pay the cost of performing the mandated activity or service for the period of time during which the activity or service is required to be performed.

Section 9. Recall of Elected County Officials

A. An elected official of a county is subject to recall by the voters of the county. Subject to the provisions of Subsection B of this section, a petition for a recall election shall cite grounds of malfeasance or misfeasance in office or violation of the oath of office by the official concerned. The cited grounds shall be based upon acts or failures to act occurring during the current term of the official sought to be recalled. The recall petition shall be signed by registered voters:

(1) of the county if the official sought to be recalled was elected at-large; or

(2) of the district from which the official sought to be recalled was elected; and

(3) not less in number than thirty-three and one-third percent of the number of persons who voted in the election for the office in the last preceding general election at which the office was voted upon.

B. Prior to and as a condition of circulating a petition for recall pursuant to the provisions of Subsection A of this section, the factual allegations supporting the grounds of malfeasance or misfeasance in office or violation of the oath of office stated in the petition shall be presented to the district court for the county in which the recall is proposed to be conducted. The petition shall not be circulated unless, after a hearing in which the proponents of the recall effort and the official sought to be recalled are given an opportunity to present evidence, the district court determines that probable cause exists for the grounds for recall.

C. After the requirements of Subsection B of this section are fulfilled, the petition shall be circulated and filed with the county clerk for verification of the signatures, as to both number and qualifications of the persons signing. If the county clerk verifies that the requisite number of signatures of registered voters appears on the petition, the question of recall of the official shall be placed on the ballot for a special election to be called and held within ninety days or the next occurring general election if that election is to be held within less than ninety days. If at the election a majority of the votes cast on the question of recall is in favor of recall, the official who is the subject of recall is recalled from the office, and a vacancy exists. That vacancy shall be filled in the manner provided by law for filling vacancies for that office.

D. A recall election shall not be conducted after May 1 in a calendar year in which an election is to be held for the office for which the recall is sought if the official sought to be recalled is a candidate for re-election to the office. No petition for recall of an elected county official shall be submitted more than once during the term for which the official is elected.

Section 10. Urban Counties

A. A county that is less than one thousand five hundred square miles in area and has a population of three hundred thousand or more may become an urban county by the following procedure:

(1) the board of county commissioners shall appoint a charter commission consisting of not less than three persons to draft a proposed urban county charter;

(2) the proposed charter shall provide for the form and organization of the urban county government and shall designate those officers that shall be elected and those officers and employees that shall perform the duties assigned by law to county officers; and

(3) within one year after the appointment of the charter commission, the proposed charter shall be submitted to the qualified voters of the county and, if adopted by a majority of those voting, the county shall become an urban county. If, at the election or any subsequent election, the proposed charter is not adopted, then, after at least one year has elapsed after the election, pursuant to this section another charter commission may be appointed and another proposed charter may be submitted to the qualified voters for approval or disapproval.

B. An urban county may exercise all legislative powers and perform all governmental functions not expressly denied by general law or charter and may exercise all powers granted to and shall be subject to all limitations placed on municipalities by Article 9, Section 12 of the constitution of New Mexico. This grant of powers shall not include the power to enact private or civil laws except as incident to the exercise of an independent municipal power, nor shall it include the power to provide for a penalty greater than the penalty provided for a misdemeanor. No tax imposed by the governing body of an urban county, except a tax authorized by general law, shall become effective until approved by a majority vote in the urban county.

C. A charter of an urban county shall only be amended in accordance with the provisions of the charter.

D. If the charter of an urban county provides for a governing body composed of members elected by districts, a member representing a district shall be a resident and elected by the registered qualified electors of that district.

E. The purpose of this section is to provide for maximum local self-government. A liberal construction shall be given to the powers of urban counties.

F. The provisions of this section shall be self-executing.

Section 11. Single Urban Governments

A. A county that is less than one thousand five hundred square miles in area and has, at the time of this amendment, a population of three hundred thousand or more, and whether or not it is an urban county pursuant to Section 1 of this amendment, may provide for a single urban government by the following procedure:

(1) by January 1, 2003, a charter commission, composed of eleven members, shall be appointed to draft a proposed charter. Five members shall be appointed by the governing body of the county, five members shall be appointed by the municipality with a population greater than three hundred thousand and one member shall be appointed by the other ten members;

(2) the proposed charter shall:

(a) provide for the form and organization of the single urban government;

(b) designate those officers that shall be elected and those officers and employees that shall perform the duties assigned by law to county officers;

(c) provide for a transition period for elected county and city officials whose terms have not expired on the effective date of the charter; and

(d) provide for a transition period, no less than one year, to ensure the continuation of government services; and

(3) within one year after the appointment of the charter commission, the proposed charter shall be submitted to the qualified voters and, if adopted by a majority of those voters, the municipalities in that county with a population greater than ten thousand shall be disincorporated and the county shall be governed by a single urban government. If the proposed charter is not adopted by a majority of the qualified voters, then another charter commission shall be appointed and another election, within twelve months of the previous election, shall be held. If the proposed charter is not adopted by a majority of the qualified voters at the second or any subsequent election, then after at least two years have elapsed after the election, pursuant to this section another charter commission may be appointed and another proposed charter may be submitted to the qualified voters for approval or disapproval. As used in this paragraph, "qualified voter" means a registered voter of the county.

B. Upon the adoption of a charter pursuant to Subsection A of this section, any municipality within the county with a population greater than ten thousand is disincorporated and no future municipalities shall be incorporated. A county that adopts a charter pursuant to this section may exercise those powers granted to urban counties by Section 1 of this amendment and is subject to the limitations imposed upon urban counties by that section. A county that adopts a charter pursuant to this section has the same power to enact taxes as any other county and as any municipality had before being disincorporated pursuant to this section.

C. A municipality, with a population of ten thousand or less, in a county that has adopted a charter pursuant to this section may become a part of the single urban government by a vote of a majority of the qualified voters within the municipality voting in an election held upon the filing of a petition containing the signatures of ten percent of the registered voters of that municipality. If a majority of the voters elect to become a part of the single urban government, then the municipality is disincorporated.

D. All property, debts, employees, records and contracts of a municipality disincorporated pursuant to this section shall be transferred to the county and become the property, debts, employees, records and contracts of the county. The rights of a municipality, disincorporated pursuant to this section, to receive taxes, fees, distributions or any other thing of value shall be transferred to the county. Any law granting any power or authorizing any distribution to a municipality disincorporated pursuant to this section shall be interpreted as granting the power or authorizing the distribution to the county.

E. The provisions of this section shall be self-executing.

ARTICLE XI: CORPORATIONS OTHER THAN MUNICIPAL

Section 1. Creation and composition of public regulation commission

The "public regulation commission" is created. The commission shall consist of five members elected from districts provided by law for staggered four-year terms beginning on January 1 of the year following their election; provided that those chosen at the first general election after the adoption of this section shall immediately classify themselves by lot, so that two of them shall hold office for two years and three of them for four years; and further provided that, after serving two terms, members shall be ineligible to hold office as a commission member until one full term has intervened. The legislature shall provide, by law, increased qualifications for commissioners and continuing education requirements for commissioners. The increased qualifications provided by this 2012 amendment shall apply to public regulation commissioners elected at the general election in 2014 and subsequent elections and to commissioners appointed to fill a vacancy at any time after July 1, 2013. No commissioner or candidate for the commission shall accept anything of value from a person or entity whose charges for services to the public are regulated by the commission.

Section 2. Responsibilities of Public Regulation Commission

The public regulation commission shall have responsibility for regulating public utilities, including electric, natural gas and water companies; transportation companies, including common and contract carriers; transmission and pipeline companies, including telephone, telegraph and information transmission companies; insurance companies and others engaged in risk assumption; and other public service companies in such manner as the legislature shall provide. The public regulation commission shall have responsibility for regulating insurance companies and others engaged in risk assumption as provided by law until July 1, 2013.

Section 3-12.

Repealed.

Section 13. General Corporation Laws

The legislature shall provide for the organization of corporations by general law. All laws relating to corporations may be altered, amended or repealed by the legislature, at any time, when necessary for the public good and general welfare, and all corporations, doing business in this state, may, as to such business, be regulated, limited or restrained by laws not in conflict with the constitution of the United States or of this constitution.

Section 14. Corporations Subject to Police Power

The police power of this state is supreme over all corporations as well as individuals.

Section 15-17.

Repealed.

Section 18. Eminent Domain of Corporate Property

The right of eminent domain shall never be so abridged or construed as to prevent the legislature from taking the property and franchises of incorporated companies and subjecting them to the public use, the same as the property of individuals.

Section 19. Chartering corporations

The secretary of state shall have responsibility for chartering corporations in such a manner as the legislature shall provide.

Section 20. Creation of Office of Superintendent of Insurance

A. The office of "superintendent of insurance" is created as of July 1, 2013. The superintendent of insurance shall regulate insurance companies and others engaged in risk assumption in such manner as provided by law. The superintendent of insurance shall be appointed by the insurance nominating committee and serve for such terms as may be provided by law; provided that the term of the first superintendent of insurance appointed pursuant to this 2012 amendment shall begin on July 1, 2013 and end on December 31, 2015.

B. The insurance nominating committee shall be appointed and have such qualifications as may be provided by law. The insurance nominating committee shall evaluate applications for superintendent of insurance in accordance with qualifications for superintendent of insurance established by law.

ARTICLE XII: EDUCATION

Section 1. Free Public Schools

A uniform system of free public schools sufficient for the education of, and open to, all the children of school age in the state shall be established and maintained.

Section 2. Permanent School Fund

The permanent school fund of the state shall consist of the proceeds of sales of Sections Two, Sixteen, Thirty-Two and Thirty-Six in each township of the state, or the lands selected in lieu thereof; the proceeds of sales of all lands that have been or may hereafter be granted to the state not otherwise appropriated by the terms and conditions of the grant; such portion of the proceeds of sales of land of the United States within the state as has been or may be granted by congress; all earnings, including interest, dividends and capital gains from investment of the permanent school fund; also all other grants, gifts and devises made to the state, the purpose of which is not otherwise specified.

Section 3. Control of Constitutional Educational Institutions; Use of State Land Proceeds and Other Educational Funds

The schools, colleges, universities and other educational institutions provided for by this constitution shall forever remain under the exclusive control of the state, and no part of the proceeds arising from the sale or disposal of any lands granted to the state by congress, or any other funds appropriated, levied or collected for educational purposes, shall be used for the support of any sectarian, denominational or private school, college or university.

Section 4. Current School Fund

All forfeitures, unless otherwise provided by law, and all fines collected under general laws; the net proceeds of property that may come to the state by escheat; the rentals of all school lands and other lands granted to the state, the disposition of which is not otherwise provided for by the terms of the grant or by act of congress shall constitute the current school fund of the state.

Section 5. Compulsory School Attendance

Every child of school age and of sufficient physical and mental ability shall be required to attend a public or other school during such period and for such time as may be prescribed by law.

Section 6. Public Education Department; Public Education Commission

A. There is hereby created a "public education department" and a "public education commission" that shall have such powers and duties as provided by law. The department shall be a cabinet department headed by a secretary of public education who is a qualified, experienced educator who shall be appointed by the governor and confirmed by the senate.

B. Ten members of the public education commission shall be elected for staggered terms of four years as provided by law. Commission members shall be residents of the public education commission district from which they are elected. Change of residence of a commission member to a place outside the district from which he was elected shall automatically terminate the term of that member.

C. The governor shall fill vacancies on the commission by appointment of a resident from the district in which the vacancy occurs until the next regular election for membership on the commission.

D. The secretary of public education shall have administrative and regulatory powers and duties, including all functions relating to the distribution of school funds and financial accounting for the public schools to be performed as provided by law.

E. The elected members of the 2003 state board of education shall constitute the public education commission, if this amendment is approved, until their terms expire and the districts from which the state board of education were elected shall constitute the state public education commission districts until changed by law.

Section 7. Investment of Permanent School Fund

A. As used in this section, "fund" means the permanent school fund described in Article 12, Section 2 of this constitution and all other permanent funds derived from lands granted or confirmed to the state by the act of congress of June 20, 1910, entitled "An act to enable the people of New Mexico to form a constitution and state government and be admitted into the union on an equal footing with the original states."

B. The fund shall be invested by the state investment officer in accordance with policy regulations promulgated by the state investment council.

C. In making investments, the state investment officer, under the supervision of the state investment council, shall invest and manage the fund in accordance with the Uniform Prudent Investor Act.

D. The legislature may establish criteria for investing the fund if the criteria are enacted by a three-fourths vote of the members elected to each house, but investment of the fund is subject to the following restrictions:

(1) not more than sixty-five percent of the book value of the fund shall be invested at any given time in corporate stocks;

(2) not more than ten percent of the voting stock of a corporation shall be held; and

(3) stocks eligible for purchase shall be restricted to those stocks of businesses listed upon a national stock exchange or included in a nationally recognized list of stocks;

E. All additions to the fund and all earnings, including interest, dividends and capital gains from investment of the fund shall be credited to the fund.

F. Except as provided in Subsection G of this section, the annual distributions from the fund shall be five percent of the average of the year-end market values of the fund for the immediately preceding five calendar years.

G. In addition to the annual distribution made pursuant to Subsection F of this section, unless suspended pursuant to Subsection H of this section, an additional annual distribution shall be made pursuant to the following schedule; provided that no distribution shall be made pursuant to the provisions of this subsection in any fiscal year if the average of the year-end market values of the fund for the immediately preceding five calendar years is less than ten billion dollars ($10,000,000,000):

(1) in fiscal years 2005 through 2012, an amount equal to eight-tenths percent of the average of the year-end market values of the fund for the immediately preceding five calendar years; provided that any additional distribution from the permanent school fund pursuant to this paragraph shall be used to implement and maintain educational reforms as provided by law; and

(2) in fiscal years 2013 through 2016, an amount equal to one-half percent of the average of the year-end market values of the fund for the immediately preceding five calendar years; provided that any additional distribution from the permanent school fund pursuant to this paragraph shall be used to implement and maintain educational reforms as provided by law.

H. The legislature, by a three-fifths' vote of the members elected to each house, may suspend any additional distribution provided for in Subsection G of this section.

Section 8. Teachers to Learn English and Spanish

The legislature shall provide for the training of teachers in the normal schools or otherwise so that they may become proficient in both the English and Spanish languages, to qualify them to teach Spanish-speaking pupils and students in the public schools and educational institutions of the state, and shall provide proper means and methods to facilitate the teaching of the English language and other branches of learning to such pupils and students.

Section 9. Religious Tests in Schools

No religious test shall ever be required as a condition of admission into the public schools or any educational institution of this state, either as a teacher or student, and no teacher or student of such school or institution shall ever be required to attend or participate in any religious service whatsoever.

Section 10. Educational Rights of Children of Spanish Descent

Children of Spanish descent in the state of New Mexico shall never be denied the right and privilege of admission and attendance in the public schools or other public educational institutions of the state, and they shall never be classed in separate schools, but shall forever enjoy perfect equality with other children in all public schools and educational institutions of the state, and the legislature shall provide penalties for the violation of this section. This section shall never be amended except upon a vote of the people of this state, in an election at which at least three-fourths of the electors voting in the whole state and at least two-thirds of those voting in each county in the state shall vote for such amendment.

Section 11. State Educational Institutions

The university of New Mexico, at Albuquerque; the New Mexico state university, near Las Cruces, formerly known as New Mexico college of agriculture and mechanic arts; the New Mexico highlands university, at Las Vegas, formerly known as New Mexico normal university; the western New Mexico university, at Silver City, formerly known as New Mexico western college and New Mexico normal school; the eastern New Mexico university, at Portales, formerly known as eastern New Mexico normal school; the New Mexico institute of mining and technology, at Socorro, formerly known as New Mexico school of mines; the New Mexico military institute, at Roswell, formerly known as New Mexico military institute; the New Mexico school for the blind and visually impaired, at Alamogordo, formerly known as New Mexico school for the visually handicapped; the New Mexico school for the deaf, at Santa Fe, formerly known as New Mexico asylum for the deaf and dumb; the northern New Mexico state school, at El Rito, formerly known as Spanish-American school; are hereby confirmed as state educational institutions. All lands, together with the natural products thereof and the money proceeds of any of the lands and products, held in trust for the institutions, respectively, under their former names, and all properties heretofore granted to, or owned by, or which may hereafter be granted or conveyed to, the institutions respectively, under their former names, shall, in like manner as heretofore, be held in trust for, or owned by or be considered granted to, the institutions individually under their names as hereinabove adopted and confirmed. The appropriations made and which may hereafter be made to the state by the United States for agriculture and mechanical colleges and experiment stations in connection therewith shall be paid to the New Mexico state university, formerly known as New Mexico college of agriculture and mechanic arts.

Section 12. Acceptance and Use of Enabling Act Educational Grants

All lands granted under the provisions of the act of congress, entitled, "An act to enable the people of New Mexico to form a constitution and state government and be admitted into the union on an equal footing with the original states; and to enable the people of Arizona to form a constitution and state government and be admitted into the union on an equal footing with the original states," for the purposes of said several institutions are hereby accepted and confirmed to said institutions, and shall be exclusively used for the purposes for which they were granted; provided, that one hundred and seventy thousand acres of the land granted by said act for normal school purposes are hereby equally apportioned between said three normal institutions, and the remaining thirty thousand acres thereof is reserved for a normal school which shall be established by the legislature and located in one of the counties of Union, Quay, Curry, Roosevelt, Chaves or Eddy.

Section 13. Board of Regents for Educational Institutions

A. The legislature shall provide for the control and management of each of the institutions, except the university of New Mexico, by a board of regents for each institution, consisting of five members, four of whom shall be qualified electors of the state of New Mexico, one of whom shall be a member of the student body of the institution and no more than three of whom at the time of their appointment shall be members of the same political party; provided, however, that the student body member provision in this subsection shall not apply to the New Mexico school for the deaf, the New Mexico military institute, or the New Mexico school for the blind and visually impaired, and for each of those three institutions all five members of the board of regents shall be qualified electors of the state of New Mexico.

B. The governor shall nominate and by and with the consent of the senate shall appoint the members of each board of regents for each of the institutions. The terms of non-student members shall be for staggered terms of six years, and the terms of student members shall be two years.

C. The governor shall select, with the advice and consent of the senate, a student member from a list provided by the president of the institution. In making the list, the president of the institution shall give due consideration to the recommendations of the student body president of the institution. Following the approval by the voters of this 2014 amendment and upon the first vacancy of a position on the northern New Mexico state school board of regents, the governor shall nominate and by and with the consent of the senate shall appoint a student member to serve a two-year term.

D. The legislature shall provide for the control and management of the university of New Mexico by a board of regents consisting of seven members, six of whom shall be qualified electors of the state of New Mexico, one of whom shall be a member of the student body of the university of New Mexico and no more than four of whom at the time of their appointment shall be members of the same political party. The governor shall nominate and by and with the consent of the senate shall appoint the members of the board of regents. The present five members shall serve out their present terms. The two additional members shall be appointed in 1987 for terms of six years. Following the approval by the voters of this amendment and upon the first vacancy of a position held by a non-student member on the university of New Mexico's board of regents, the governor shall nominate and by and with the consent of the senate shall appoint a student member to serve a two-year term. The governor shall select, with the advice and consent of the senate, a student member from a list provided by the president of the university of New Mexico. In making the list, the president of the university of New

Mexico shall give due consideration to the recommendations of the student body president of the university.

E. Members of the board shall not be removed except for incompetence, neglect of duty or malfeasance in office. Provided, however, no removal shall be made without notice of hearing and an opportunity to be heard having first been given such member. The supreme court of the state of New Mexico is hereby given exclusive original jurisdiction over proceedings to remove members of the board under such rules as it may promulgate, and its decision in connection with such matters shall be final.

Section 14. Recall of Local School Board Members

Any elected local school board member is subject to recall by the voters of the school district from which elected. A petition for a recall election must cite grounds of malfeasance or misfeasance in office or violation of the oath of office by the member concerned. The recall petition shall be signed by registered voters not less in number than thirty-three and one-third percent of those who voted for the office at the last preceding election at which the office was voted upon. Procedures for filing petitions and for determining validity of signatures shall be as provided by law. If at the special election a majority of the votes cast on the question of recall are in favor thereof, the local school board member is recalled from office and the vacancy shall be filled as provided by law.

Section 15. Local School Boards Having Seven Single-Member Districts

In those local school districts having a population of more than two hundred thousand, as shown by the most recent decennial census, the qualified electors of the districts may choose to have a local school board composed of seven members, residents of and elected from single member districts.

If a majority of the qualified electors voting in such a district election vote to have a seven-member board, the school district shall be divided into seven local school board member districts which shall be compact, contiguous and as nearly equal in population as possible. One school board member shall reside within, and be elected from each local school board member district. Change of residence to a place outside the district from which a school board member was elected shall automatically terminate the service of that school board member and the office shall be declared vacant.

The school board member districts shall be established by resolution of the local school board with the approval of the state legislature, and may be changed once after each federal decennial census by the local school board with the approval of the state legislature.

The elections required under this amendment shall be called and conducted as provided by law for other local school board elections. The state board of education shall, by resolution, establish the terms of the first board elected after the creation of such a seven-member board.

ARTICLE XIII: PUBLIC LANDS

Section 1. Disposition of State Lands

All lands belonging to the territory of New Mexico, and all lands granted, transferred or confirmed to the state by congress, and all lands hereafter acquired, are declared to be public lands of the state to be held or disposed of as may be provided by law for the purposes for which they have been or may be granted, donated or otherwise acquired; provided, that such of school Sections Two, Thirty-Two, Sixteen and Thirty-Six as are not contiguous to other state lands shall not be sold within the period of ten years next after the admission of New Mexico as a state for less than ten dollars [($10.00)] per acre.

Section 2. Duties of Land Commissioner

The commissioner of public lands shall select, locate, classify and have the direction, control, care and disposition of all public lands, under the provisions of the acts of congress relating thereto and such regulations as may be provided by law.

Section 3. Patents for Public Lands

The provisions of the Enabling Act (36 Stat. 557, 563) which prohibit the granting of a patent for a portion of a tract of public lands under sales contract because the full consideration for the entire tract is not or was not paid, are waived with respect to the following sales:

A. sale of a portion of a tract under sales contract, if the patent to that portion was issued on or before September 4, 1956;

B. sale of a portion of a tract under sales contract, if the right to purchase the portion is derived from an assignment made on or before September 4, 1956; or

C. sale of a portion of a tract under sales contract, or under a contract entered into in substitution of such contract, if the right to purchase all other portions of the tract were assigned or relinquished on or before September 4, 1956 by the person holding the contract.

The legislature may enact laws to carry out the purposes of this amendment.

ARTICLE XIV: PUBLIC INSTITUTIONS

Section 1. State Institutions

The penitentiary at Santa Fe, the miner's hospital at Raton, the New Mexico state hospital at Las Vegas, the New Mexico boys' school at Springer, the girls' welfare home at Albuquerque, the Carrie Tingley crippled children's hospital at Truth or Consequences and the Los Lunas mental hospital at Los Lunas are hereby confirmed as state institutions.

Section 2. Federal Land Grants and Donations

All lands which have been or which may be granted to the state by congress for the purpose of said several institutions are hereby accepted for said several institutions with all other grants, donations or devices for the benefit of the same and shall be exclusively used for the purpose for which they were or may be granted, donated or devised.

Section 3. Control and Management

Each of said institutions shall be under such control and management as may be provided by law.

ARTICLE XV: AGRICULTURE AND CONSERVATION

Section 1. Department of Agriculture

There shall be a department of agriculture which shall be under the control of the board of regents of the college of agriculture and mechanic arts; and the legislature shall provide lands and funds necessary for experimental farming and demonstrating by said department.

Section 2. Forest Fire Prevention

The police power of the state shall extend to such control of private forest lands as shall be necessary for the prevention and suppression of forest fires.

ARTICLE XVI: IRRIGATION AND WATER RIGHTS

Section 1. Existing Water Rights Confirmed

All existing rights to the use of any waters in this state for any useful or beneficial purpose are hereby recognized and confirmed.

Section 2. Appropriation of Water

The unappropriated water of every natural stream, perennial or torrential, within the state of New Mexico, is hereby declared to belong to the public and to be subject to appropriation for beneficial use, in accordance with the laws of the state. Priority of appropriation shall give the better right.

Section 3. Beneficial Use of Water

Beneficial use shall be the basis, the measure and the limit of the right to the use of water.

Section 4. Drainage Districts and Systems

The legislature is authorized to provide by law for the organization and operation of drainage districts and systems.

Section 5. Appeals in Matters Relating to Water Rights

In any appeal to the district court from the decision, act or refusal to act of any state executive officer or body in matters relating to water rights, the proceeding upon appeal shall be de novo as cases originally docketed in the district court unless otherwise provided by law.

Section 6. Water Trust Fund

A. The "water trust fund" is created in the state treasury to conserve and protect the water resources of New Mexico and to ensure that New Mexico has the water it needs for a strong and vibrant future. The purpose of the fund shall be to secure a supply of clean and safe water for New Mexico's residents. The fund shall consist of money appropriated, donated or otherwise accrued to the fund. Money in the fund shall be invested by the state investment officer as land grant permanent funds are invested, and there shall be strict accountability and oversight measures as provided by the state investment council to ensure appropriate safety of and return on investments. Earnings from investment of the fund shall be credited to the fund. Money in the fund shall not revert or be expended for any purpose, but an annual distribution shall be made to the water project fund, which shall be used only to support critically needed projects that preserve and protect New Mexico's water supply and is in accordance with Subsection B of this section.

B. On July 1, 2008 and each fiscal year thereafter, an annual distribution shall be made from the water trust fund pursuant to law, and that distribution shall then be appropriated by the legislature only for water projects consistent with a state water plan and as otherwise provided by law.

ARTICLE XVII: MINES AND MINING

Section 1. Inspector of Mines

There shall be a state mine inspector who shall be appointed by the governor, by and with the advice and consent of the senate, for a term of four years, and whose duties and salary shall be as prescribed by law. The legislature may pass laws prescribing reasonable qualifications for the state mine inspector and deputy mine inspectors, and current legislative enactments prescribing such qualifications are declared to be in full force and effect.

Section 2. Mining Regulations; Employment of Children under Fourteen

The legislature shall enact laws requiring the proper ventilation of mines, the construction and maintenance of escapement shafts or slopes, and the adoption and use of appliances necessary to protect the health and secure the safety of employees therein. No children under the age of fourteen years shall be employed in mines.

ARTICLE XVIII: MILITIA

Section 1. Composition, Name and Commander in Chief of Militia

The militia of this state shall consist of all able-bodied male citizens between the ages of eighteen and forty-five, except such as are exempt by laws of the United States or of this state. The organized militia shall be called the "national guard of New Mexico," of which the governor shall be the commander in chief.

Section 2. Organization, Discipline and Equipment of Militia

The legislature shall provide for the organization, discipline and equipment of the militia, which shall conform as nearly as practicable to the organization, discipline and equipment of the regular army of the United States, and shall provide for the maintenance thereof.

ARTICLE XIX: AMENDMENTS

Section 1. Proposing and Ratifying Amendments

An amendment or amendments to this constitution may be proposed in either house of the legislature at a regular session; and if a majority of all members elected to each of the two houses voting separately votes in favor thereof, the proposed amendment or amendments shall be entered on their respective journals with the yeas and nays thereon.

An amendment or amendments may also be proposed by an independent commission established by law for that purpose, and the amendment or amendments shall be submitted to the legislature for its review in accordance with the provisions of this section.

The secretary of state shall cause any such amendment or amendments to be published in at least one newspaper in every county of the state, where a newspaper is published once each week, for four consecutive weeks, in English and Spanish when newspapers in both of said languages are published in such counties, the last publication to be not more than two weeks prior to the election at which time said amendment or amendments shall be submitted to the electors of the state for their approval or rejection; and shall further provide notice of the content and purpose of legislatively approved constitutional amendments in both English and Spanish to inform electors about the amendments in the time and manner provided by law. The secretary of state shall also make reasonable efforts to provide notice of the content and purpose of legislatively approved constitutional amendments in indigenous languages and to minority language groups to inform electors about the amendments. Amendments approved by the legislature shall be voted upon at the next regular election held after the adjournment of that legislature or at a special election to be held not less than six months after the adjournment of that legislature, at such time and in such manner as the legislature may by law provide. An amendment that is ratified by a majority of the electors voting on the amendment shall become part of this constitution.

If two or more amendments are initiated by the legislature, they shall be so submitted as to enable the electors to vote on each of them separately. Amendments initiated by an independent commission created by law for that purpose may be submitted to the legislature separately or as a single ballot question, and any such commission-initiated amendments that are not substantially altered by the legislature may be submitted to the electors in the separate or single ballot question form recommended by the commission. No amendment shall restrict the rights created by Sections One and Three of Article VII hereof, on elective franchise, and Sections Eight and Ten of Article XII hereof, on education, unless it be proposed by vote of three-fourths of the members elected to each house and be ratified by a vote of the people of this state in an election at which at least three-fourths of the electors voting on the amendment vote in favor of that amendment.

Section 2. Constitutional Conventions

Whenever the legislature, by a two-thirds vote of the members elected to each house, deems it necessary to call a convention to revise or amend this constitution, they shall submit the question of calling such convention to the electors at the next general election, and if a majority of all the electors voting on such questions at said election in the state votes in favor of calling a convention, the legislature shall, at the next session, provide by law for calling the same. Such convention shall consist of at least as many delegates as there are members of the house of representatives.

Revisions or amendments proposed by a constitutional convention shall be submitted to the voters of the state at an election held on a date set by the convention. The revisions or amendments proposed by the convention may be submitted in whole or in part, or with alternatives, as determined by the convention. If a majority vote favors a proposal or alternative, it is adopted and becomes effective thirty days after the certification of the election returns unless otherwise provided by the convention.

Section 3. Initiative Restricted

If this constitution be in any way so amended as to allow laws to be enacted by direct vote of the electors the laws which may be so enacted shall be only such as might be enacted by the legislature under the provisions of this constitution.

Section 4. Amendment of Compact with United States

When the United States shall consent thereto, the legislature, by a majority vote of the members in each house, may submit to the people the question of amending any provision of Article XXI of this constitution on compact with the United States to the extent allowed by the act of congress permitting the same, and if a majority of the qualified electors who vote upon any such amendment shall vote in favor thereof the said article shall be thereby amended accordingly.

ARTICLE XX: MISCELLANEOUS

Section 1. Oath of Officer

Every person elected or appointed to any office shall, before entering upon his duties, take and subscribe to an oath or affirmation that he will support the constitution of the United States and the constitution and laws of this state, and that he will faithfully and impartially discharge the duties of his office to the best of his ability.

Section 2. Tenure of Office

Every officer, unless removed, shall hold his office until his successor has duly qualified.

Section 3. Date Terms of Office Begin

The term of office of every state, county or district officer, except those elected at the first election held under this constitution, and those elected to fill vacancies, shall commence on the first day of January next after his election.

Section 4. Vacancies in Offices of District Attorney or County Commissioner

If a vacancy occurs in the office of district attorney or county commissioner, the governor shall fill such vacancy by appointment, and such appointee shall hold such office until the next general election. His successor shall be chosen at such election and shall hold his office until the expiration of the original term.

Section 5. Interim Appointments

If, while the senate is not in session, a vacancy occur in any office the incumbent of which was appointed by the governor by and with the advice and consent of the senate, the governor shall appoint some qualified person to fill the same until the next session of the senate; and shall then appoint by and with the advice and consent of the senate some qualified person to fill said office for the period of the unexpired term.

Section 6. Date of General Elections

General elections shall be held in the state on the Tuesday after the first Monday in November in each even-numbered year.

Section 7. Canvass of Returns for Officers Elected by More Than One County

The returns of all elections for officers who are chosen by the electors of more than one county shall be canvassed by the county canvassing board of each county as to the vote within their respective counties. Said board shall immediately certify the number of votes received by each candidate for such office within such county, to the state canvassing board herein established, which shall canvass and declare the result of the election.

Section 8. First National Election

In the event that New Mexico is admitted into the union as a state prior to the Tuesday next after the first Monday in November in the year nineteen hundred and twelve, and if no provision has been made by the state legislature therefore, an election shall be held in the state on the said Tuesday next after the first Monday in November, nineteen hundred and twelve, for the election of presidential electors; and such election shall be held as herein provided for the election upon the ratification of this constitution, and the returns thereof made to, and canvassed and certified by, the state canvassing board as herein provided in case of the election of state officers.

Section 9. State Officers Limited to Salaries

No officer of the state who receives a salary, shall accept or receive to his own use any compensation, fees, allowance or emoluments for or on account of his office, in any form whatever, except the salary provided by law.

Section 10. Child Labor

The legislature shall enact suitable laws for the regulation of the employment of children.

Section 11. Women as Public Officers

Women may hold the office of notary public and such other appointive offices as may be provided by law.

Section 12. Publication of Laws in English and Spanish

For the first twenty years after this constitution goes into effect all laws passed by the legislature shall be published in both the English and Spanish languages and thereafter such publication shall be made as the legislature may provide.

Section 13. Sacramental Wines

The use of wines solely for sacramental purposes under church authority at any place within the state shall never be prohibited.

Section 14. Public Officers Barred from Using Railroad Passes

It shall not be lawful for the governor, any member of the state board of equalization, any member of the corporation commission [public regulation commission], any judge of the supreme or district court, any district attorney, any county commissioner or any county assessor, during his term of office to accept, hold or use any free pass; or purchase, receive or accept transportation over any railroad within this state for himself or his family upon terms not open to the general public; and any person violating the provisions hereof shall, upon conviction in a court of a competent jurisdiction, be punished as provided in Sections Thirty-Seven and Forty of the article on Legislative Department in this constitution.

Section 15. Penitentiary to Be Reformatory and Industrial School; Labor by Inmates

The penitentiary is a reformatory and an industrial school, and all persons confined therein shall, so far as consistent with discipline and the public interest, be employed in some beneficial industry; and where a convict has a dependent family, his net earnings shall be paid to said family if necessary for their support.

Section 16. Railroad's Liability to Employees

Every person, receiver or corporation owning or operating a railroad within this state shall be liable in damages for injury to, or the death of, any person in its employ, resulting from the negligence, in whole or in part, of said owner or operator, or of any of the officers, agents or employees thereof, or by reason of any defect or insufficiency, due to its negligence, in whole or in part, in its cars, engines, appliances, machinery, track, roadbed, works or other equipment.

An action for negligently causing the death of an employee as above provided shall be maintained by the executor or administrator for the benefit of the employee's surviving widow or husband and children; or if none, then his parents; or if none, then the next of kin dependent upon said deceased. The amount recovered may be distributed as provided by law. Any contract or agreement made in advance of such injury with any employee waiving or limiting any right to recover such damages shall be void.

This provision shall not be construed to affect the provisions of Section Two of Article Twenty-Two of this constitution, being the article upon Schedule.

Section 17.

Repealed.

Section 18. Leasing of Convict Labor Prohibited

The leasing of convict labor by the state is hereby prohibited.

Section 19. Eight-Hour Day in Public Employment

Eight hours shall constitute a day's work in all cases of employment by and on behalf of the state or any county or municipality thereof.

Section 20. Waiver of Indictment; Proceedings on Information

Any person held by a committing magistrate to await the action of the grand jury on a charge of felony or other infamous crime, may in open court with the consent of the court and the district attorney, to be entered upon the record, waive indictment and plead to an information in the form of an indictment filed by the district attorney, and further proceedings shall then be had upon said information with like force and effect as though it were an indictment duly returned by the grand jury.

Section 21. Pollution Control

The protection of the state's beautiful and healthful environment is hereby declared to be of fundamental importance to the public interest, health, safety and the general welfare. The legislature shall provide for control of pollution and control of despoilment of the air, water and other natural resources of this state, consistent with the use and development of these resources for the maximum benefit of the people.

Section 22. Public Employees and Educational Retirement Systems Trust Funds; Expenditures and Encumbrance Prohibited; Administration; Vesting of Property Rights

A. All funds, assets, proceeds, income, contributions, gifts and payments from any source whatsoever paid into or held by a public employees retirement system or an educational retirement system created by the laws of this state shall be held by each respective system in a trust fund to be administered and invested by each respective system for the sole and exclusive benefit of the members, retirees and other beneficiaries of that system. Expenditures from a system trust fund shall only be made for the benefit of the trust beneficiaries and for expenses of administering the system. A system trust fund shall never be used, diverted, loaned, assigned, pledged, invested, encumbered or appropriated for any other purpose. To the extent consistent with the provisions of this section, each trust fund shall be invested and the systems administered as provided by law.

B. The retirement board of the public employees retirement system and the board of the educational retirement system shall be the trustees for their respective systems and have the sole and exclusive fiduciary duty and responsibility for administration and investment of the trust fund held by their respective systems.

C. A retirement board shall have the sole and exclusive power and authority to adopt actuarial assumptions for its system based upon the recommendations made by an independent actuary with whom it contracts. The legislature shall not enact any law that increases the benefits paid by the system in any manner or changes the funding formula for a retirement plan unless adequate funding is provided.

D. Upon meeting the minimum service requirements of an applicable retirement plan created by law for employees of the state or any of its political subdivisions or institutions, a member of a plan shall acquire a vested property right with due process protections under the applicable provisions of the New Mexico and United States constitutions.

E. Nothing in this section shall be construed to prohibit modifications to retirement plans that enhance or preserve the actuarial soundness of an affected trust fund or individual retirement plan.

ARTICLE XXI: COMPACT WITH THE UNITED STATES

Section 1. Religious Toleration; Polygamy

Perfect toleration of religious sentiment shall be secured, and no inhabitant of this state shall ever be molested in person or property on account of his or her mode of religious worship. Polygamous or plural marriages and polygamous cohabitation are forever prohibited.

Section 2. Control of Unappropriated or Indian Lands; Taxation of Federal Government, Nonresident and Indian Property

The people inhabiting this state do agree and declare that they forever disclaim all right and title to the unappropriated and ungranted public lands lying within the boundaries thereof, and to all lands lying within said boundaries owned or held by any Indian or Indian tribes, the right or title to which shall have been acquired through the United States, or any prior sovereignty; and that until the title of such Indian or Indian tribes shall have been extinguished the same shall be and remain subject to the disposition and under the absolute jurisdiction and control of the congress of the United States; and that the lands and other property belonging to citizens of the United States residing without this state shall never be taxed at a higher rate than the lands and other property belonging to residents thereof; that no taxes shall be imposed by this state upon lands or property therein belonging to or which may hereafter be acquired by the United States or reserved for its use; but nothing herein shall preclude this state from taxing as other lands and property are taxed, any lands and other property outside of an Indian reservation, owned or held by any Indian, save and except such lands as have been granted or acquired as aforesaid, or as may be granted or confirmed to any Indian or Indians under any act of congress; but all such lands shall be exempt from taxation by this state so long and to such extent as the congress of the United States has prescribed or may hereafter prescribe.

Section 3. Assumption of Territorial Debts

The debts and liabilities of the territory of New Mexico and the debts of the counties thereof, which were valid and subsisting on the twentieth day of June, nineteen hundred and ten, are hereby assumed and shall be paid by this state; and this state shall, as to all such debts and liabilities, be subrogated to all the rights, including rights of indemnity and reimbursement, existing in favor of said territory or of any of the several counties thereof on said date. Nothing in this article shall be construed as validating or in any manner legalizing any territorial, county, municipal or other bonds, warrants, obligations or evidences of indebtedness of, or claims against, said territory or any of the counties or municipalities thereof which now are or may be, at the time this state is admitted, invalid and illegal; nor shall the legislature of this state pass any law in any manner validating or legalizing the same.

Section 4. Public Schools

Provision shall be made for the establishment and maintenance of a system of public schools which shall be open to all the children of the state and free from sectarian control, and said schools shall always be conducted in English.

Section 5. Suffrage

This state shall never enact any law restricting or abridging the right of suffrage on account of race, color or previous condition of servitude.

Section 6. Capital

The capital of this state shall, until changed by the electors voting at an election provided for by the legislature of this state for that purpose, be at the city of Santa Fe, but no such election shall be called or provided for prior to the thirty-first day of December, nineteen hundred and twenty-five.

Section 7. Reclamation Projects

There are hereby reserved to the United States, with full acquiescence of the people of this state, all rights and powers for the carrying out of the provisions by the United States of the act of congress, entitled, "An act appropriating the receipts from the sale and disposal of public lands in certain states and territories to the construction of irrigation works for the reclamation of arid lands," approved June seventeenth, nineteen hundred and two, and acts amendatory thereof or supplementary thereto, to the same extent as if this state had remained a territory.

Section 8. Allotted Indian Lands Subject to Federal Liquor Control

Whenever hereafter any of the lands contained within Indian reservations or allotments in this state shall be allotted, sold, reserved or otherwise disposed of, they shall be subject for a period of twenty-five years after such allotment, sale, reservation or other disposal, to all the laws of the United States prohibiting the introduction of liquor into the Indian country; and the terms "Indian" and "Indian country" shall include the Pueblo Indians of New Mexico and the lands owned or occupied by them on the twentieth day of June, nineteen hundred and ten, or which are occupied by them at the time of the admission of New Mexico as a state.

Section 9. Consent to Enabling Act Provisions

This state and its people consent to all and singular the provisions of the said act of congress, approved June twentieth, nineteen hundred and ten, concerning the lands by said act granted or confirmed to this state, the terms and conditions upon which said grants and confirmations were made and the means and manner of enforcing such terms and conditions, all in every respect and particular as in said act provided.

Section 10. Compact Irrevocable

This ordinance is irrevocable without the consent of the United States and the people of this state, and no change or abrogation of this ordinance, in whole or in part, shall be made by any constitutional amendment without the consent of congress.

Section 11. Consent to Exchange of Lands

This state and its people consent to the provisions of the act of congress, approved June 15, 1926, providing for such exchanges and the governor and other state officers mentioned in said act are hereby authorized to execute the necessary instrument or instruments to effect the exchange of lands therein provided for with the government of the United States; provided that in the determination of values of the lands now owned by the state of New Mexico, the value of the lands, the timber thereon and mineral rights pertaining thereto shall control the determination of value. The legislature may enact laws for the carrying out of the provisions hereof in accordance herewith.

ARTICLE XXII: SCHEDULE

Section 1. Effective Date of Constitution

This constitution shall take effect and be in full force immediately upon the admission of New Mexico into the union as a state.

Section 2. Federal Employers' Liability Act

Until otherwise provided by law, the act of congress of the United States, entitled, "An act relating to liability of common carriers, by railroads to their employees in certain cases," approved April twenty-two, nineteen hundred and eight, and all acts amendatory thereof, shall be and remain in force in this state to the same extent that they have been in force in the territory of New Mexico.

Section 3. Federal Mining Inspection Act

Until otherwise provided by law, the act of congress, entitled, "An act for the protection of the lives of miners," approved March three, eighteen hundred and ninety-one, and all acts amendatory thereof, shall be and remain in force in this state to the same extent that they have been in force in the territory of New Mexico; the words "governor of the state," are hereby substituted for the words "governor of such organized territory," and for the words "secretary of the interior" wherever the same appear in said acts; and the chief mine inspector for the territory of New Mexico, appointed by the president of the United States, is hereby authorized to perform the duties prescribed by said acts until superseded by the "inspector of mines" appointed by the governor, as elsewhere provided by the constitution, and he shall receive the same compensation from the state, as he received from the United States.

Section 4. Territorial Laws

All laws of the territory of New Mexico in force at the time of its admission into the union as a state, not inconsistent with this constitution, shall be and remain in force as the laws of the state until they expire by their own limitation, or are altered or repealed; and all rights, actions, claims, contracts, liabilities and obligations, shall continue and remain unaffected by the change in the form of government.

Section 5. Pardons for Violation of Territorial Laws

The pardoning power herein granted shall extend to all persons who have been convicted of offenses against the laws of the territory of New Mexico.

Section 6. Territorial Property Vested in State

All property, real and personal, and all moneys, credits, claims and choses in action belonging to the territory of New Mexico, shall become the property of this state; and all debts, taxes, fines, penalties, escheats and forfeitures, which have accrued or may accrue to said territory, shall inure to this state.

Section 7. Obligations Due Territory or Subdivision

All recognizances, bonds, obligations and undertakings entered into or executed to the territory of New Mexico, or to any county, school district, municipality, officer or official board therein, shall remain valid according to the terms thereof, and may be sued upon and recovered by the proper authority under the state law.

Section 8. Territorial Judicial Process and Proceedings

All lawful process, writs, judgments, decrees, convictions and sentences issued, rendered, had or pronounced, in force at the time of the admission of the state, shall continue and remain in force to the same extent as if the change of government had not occurred, and shall be enforced and executed under the laws of the state.

Section 9. Territorial Courts and Officers; Seals

All courts existing, and all persons holding offices or appointments under authority of said territory, at the time of the admission of the state, shall continue to hold and exercise their respective jurisdictions, functions, offices and appointments until superseded by the courts, officers or authorities provided for by this constitution.

Until otherwise provided by law, the seal of the territory shall be used as the seal of the state, and the seals of the several courts, officers and official boards in the territory shall be used as the seals of the corresponding courts, officers and official boards in the state; and for any new court, office or board created by this constitution, a seal may be adopted by the judge of said court, or the incumbent of said office, or by the said board.

Section 10. Pending Actions

All suits, indictments, criminal actions, bonds, process, matters and proceedings pending in any of the courts in the territory of New Mexico at the time of the organization of the courts provided for in this constitution shall be transferred to and proceed to determination in such courts of like or corresponding jurisdiction. And all civil causes of action and criminal offenses which shall have been commenced, or indictment found, shall be subject to action, prosecution, indictment and review in the proper courts of the state, in like manner and to the same extent as if the state had been created and said courts established prior to the accrual of such causes of action and the commission of such offenses.

Section 11. Execution and Deposit of Constitution

This constitution shall be signed by the president and secretary of the constitutional convention, and such delegates as desire to sign the same, and shall be deposited in the office of the secretary of the territory where it may be signed at any time by any delegate.

Section 12. Territorial Obligations; Names of Political Subdivisions

All lawful debts and obligations of the several counties of the territory of New Mexico not assumed by the state and of the school districts, municipalities, irrigation districts and improvement districts, therein, existing at the time of its admission as a state, shall remain valid and unaffected by the change of government, until paid or refunded according to law; and all counties, municipalities and districts in said territory shall continue with the same names, boundaries and rights until changed in accordance with the constitution and laws of the state.

Section 13. Election to Ratify Constitution

This constitution shall be submitted to the people of New Mexico for ratification at an election to be held on the twenty-first day of January, nineteen hundred and eleven, at which election the qualified voters of New Mexico shall vote directly for or against the same, and the governor of the territory of New Mexico shall forthwith issue his proclamation ordering said election to be held on said day.

Except as to the manner of making returns of said election and canvassing and certifying the result thereof, said election shall be held and conducted in the manner prescribed by the laws of New Mexico now in force.

Section 14. Ballots for Ratifying Constitution

The ballots cast at said election in favor of the ratification of this constitution shall have printed or written thereon in both English and Spanish the words "For the Constitution;" and those against the ratification of the constitution shall have written or printed thereon in both English and Spanish the words "Against the Constitution;" and shall be counted and returned accordingly.

Section 15. Canvass of Ratification Election Returns

The returns of said election shall be made by the election officers direct to the secretary of the territory of New Mexico at Santa Fe, who, with the governor and the chief justice of said territory, shall constitute a canvassing board, and they, or any two of them, shall meet at said city of Santa Fe on the third Monday after said election and shall canvass the same. Said canvassing board shall make and file with the secretary of the territory of New Mexico, a certificate signed by at least two of them, setting forth the number of votes cast at said election for or against the constitution, respectively.

Section 16. Submission of Constitution to President and Congress

If a majority of the legal votes cast at said election as certified to by said canvassing board, shall be for constitution, it shall be deemed to be duly ratified by the people of New Mexico and the secretary of the territory of New Mexico shall forthwith cause to be submitted to the president of the United States and to congress for approval, a certified copy of this constitution, together with the statement of the votes cast thereon.

Section 17. Proclamation for First Election of Officers

If congress and the president approve this constitution, or if the president approves the same and congress fails to disapprove the same during the next regular session thereof, the governor of

New Mexico shall, within thirty days after receipt of notification from the president certifying said facts, issue his proclamation for an election at which officers for a full state government, including a governor, county officers, members of the state legislature, two representatives in congress to be elected at large from the state, and such other officers as this constitution prescribes, shall be chosen by the people; said election to take place not earlier than sixty days nor later than ninety days after the date of said proclamation by the governor ordering the same.

Section 18. Conduct of First State Election; Certification of Results to President

Said last-mentioned election shall be held, the returns thereof made, canvassed and certified to by the secretary of said territory, in the same manner, and under the same laws, including those as to qualifications of electors, shall be applicable thereto, as hereinbefore prescribed for holding, making of the returns, canvassing and certifying the same, of the election for the ratification or rejection of this constitution.

When said election of state and county officers, members of the legislature, representatives in congress, and other officers provided for in this constitution, shall be held and the returns thereof made, canvassed and certified as hereinbefore provided, the governor of the territory of New Mexico shall immediately certify the result of said election, as canvassed and certified as hereinbefore provided, to the president of the United States.

Section 19. First State Officers

Within thirty days after the issuance by the president of the United States of his proclamation announcing the result of said election so ascertained, all officers elected at such election, except members of the legislature, shall take the oath of office and give bond as required by this constitution or by the laws of the territory of New Mexico in case of like officers in the territory, county or district, and shall thereupon enter upon the duties of their respective offices; but the legislature may by law require such officers to give other or additional bonds as a condition of their continuance in office.

Section 20. First Legislative Session; Oaths of Members; Election of United States Senators

The governor of the state, immediately upon his qualifying and entering upon the duties of his office, shall issue his proclamation convening the legislature at the seat of government on a day to be specified therein, not less than thirty nor more than sixty days after the date of said proclamation.

The members-elect of the legislature shall meet on the day specified, take the oath required by this constitution and within ten days after organization shall proceed to the election of two senators of the United States for the state of New Mexico, in the manner prescribed by the constitution and laws of the United States; and the governor and secretary of the state of New Mexico shall certify the election of the senators and representatives in congress in the manner required by law.

Section 21. Supplementary Legislation

The legislature shall pass all necessary laws to carry into effect the provisions of this constitution.

Section 22. Terms of First Officers

The term of office of all officers elected at the election aforesaid shall commence on the date of their qualification and shall expire at the same time as if they had been elected on the Tuesday next after the first Monday of November in the year nineteen hundred and twelve.

ARTICLE XXIII: INTOXICATING LIQUORS

Repealed.

ARTICLE XXIV: LEASES ON STATE LAND

Section 1. Contracts for the Development and Production of Minerals or Development and Operation of Geothermal Steam and Waters on State Lands

Leases and other contracts, reserving a royalty to the state, for the development and production of any and all minerals or for the development and operation of geothermal steam and waters on lands granted or confirmed to the state of New Mexico by the act of congress of June 20, 1910, entitled "An act to enable the people of New Mexico to form a constitution and state government and be admitted into the union on an equal footing with the original states," may be made under such provisions relating to the necessity or requirement for or the mode and manner of appraisement, advertisement and competitive bidding, and containing such terms and provisions, as may be provided by act of the legislature; the rentals, royalties and other proceeds therefrom to be applied and conserved in accordance with the provisions of said act of congress for the support or in aid of the common schools, or for the attainment of the respective purposes for which the several grants were made.